About The Authors

Mark Cullen is Canada's leading garden expert. His education in horticulture began as a child in the family garden
business; he is now President of the Weall & Cullen Garden
Centres throughout Southern Ontario. He is the host of
CBC television's popular "Anything Grows" garden show,
the resident garden expert on CFRB Radio, and the author
of a syndicated garden column for newspapers throughout
Canada. Mark Cullen is also the author of *A Greener Thumb
— The Complete Guide to Gardening in Canada*.

Lorraine Johnson is a writer, researcher and editor who lives
and works in Toronto. She was born in Stratford, Ontario,
and raised in Galt. After graduating from the University of
Toronto, she worked in magazine and book publishing, most
recently as an editor at Penguin Books. She credits her
father (an inveterate recycler) with instilling environmental concerns in her life at an early age. She is the author of
Green Future: How to Make a World of Difference, published
by Penguin.

Lorraine Johnson is a Master Composter, trained by the
Recycling Council of Ontario through a Metro Toronto
volunteer program.

THE URBAN/SUBURBAN
COMPOSTER

THE URBAN/SUBURBAN COMPOSTER

The Complete Guide to
Backyard, Balcony, and Apartment
Composting

by Mark Cullen
and Lorraine Johnson

Illustrations by Andrew Leyerle

St. Martin's Press
New York

ISBN 0-312-10530-4

First published in Canada by Penguin Books, under the title *The Real Dirt*.
First U.S. Edition: February 1994

10 9 8 7 6 5 4 3 2 1

*My effort in this book is
dedicated to my wife and life partner, Mary.
Mother of our earthlings.*

Mark Cullen

*Again, for my father, Keith and Ross —
and for Andrew, with love.
In memory of my grandmother,
a garden enthusiast from way back.*

Lorraine Johnson

Preface

This book is an expression of something I feel very passionate about. Soil renewal.

Consider the fact that up to 40 percent of our residential curbside waste is organic matter that would compost beautifully. Instead, many of us choose to send it to the landfill where it will languish and take up space. The idea of throwing out organic waste, just to get it out of the way, is absurd.

If that isn't enough to convince you to compost, then let's take a look at the money involved. Gardeners typically enhance their soil with peat moss, composted manure, commercial fertilizers or topsoil. But these are just substitutes for the real thing — the dead and decayed plant material known as compost. It's nature's own soil enhancer and fertilizer, and it's absolutely free once the investment into a commercial composter or materials to build a bin has been made.

The miracle of life going on in the topsoil we so irreverently refer to as dirt is another compelling reason to compost. Every handful of garden dirt contains a thriving colony of more than 6,000 micro-organisms that play a vital role in the successful evolution of plant and animal life.

My passion for compost stems from observance of a very basic rule of life — put things back in their place after you're finished with them. It just doesn't make sense to remove goodness from the earth without replenishing it. Sooner or later, our soil is going to suffer — and we with it.

This book addresses the delicate business of our planet's resources and how they relate to gardens and plants. It also serves as a reminder that we have an awesome responsibility to future generations for this fragile and precious home we refer to so loosely as Mother Earth.

Mark Cullen

Acknowledgements

Many people and groups gave freely of their time and expertise. To all, many thanks: City Farmer, Tania Craan, Amy Willard Cross, Anna Scott Draper, Ecological Agriculture Projects, Albert Eggen, Frank Eggen, David Fernandez, Kristina Marie Guiguet, Tony Hamilton, Gudrun Knoessl, Michael Levenston, Carolyn McSkimming, Kate Middleton, Rod Northey, Christa Pettingill, Recycling Council of Ontario, Seattle Tilth Association, Sarah Sheard, Iris Skeoch, Michael Snyder, Lori Stoltz, Judy Vellend, Alex Wilson, and all the Master Composters.

I feel very lucky to have a family full of compost enthusiasts: my mother, Alma Johnson, whose composting experiments provided inspiration; my father, who shared his composting worms and editorial expertise; Tasha and Robert, who asked good and hard questions; Ross and Keith, long known affectionately as Rot and D.K.; Janet who takes her compost with her when she moves; Eileen and Lee.

For his skilful and beautiful illustrations, Andrew Leyerle deserves much praise and many thanks.

For their great work in promoting composting and providing composting information, I would like to thank the following non-profit groups (their addresses are in the Sources section at the back of the book and all accept donations and issue tax receipts): City Farmer, Ecological Agriculture Projects, Recycling Council of Ontario, and the Seattle Tilth Association.

Although they may not know it, the following people have been my "gardening gurus" for many years, constant sources of inspiration and information: Nancy Fleming, Mary Ellen Leyerle and Peg Livingston.

And finally, to everyone at Penguin and St. Martin's, three cheers!

Lorraine Johnson

Contents

THE URBAN/SUBURBAN
COMPOSTER

■
FOREWORD
■

Composting, the Environment and the Garden

In our society we spend a lot of time, energy, money and natural resources stopping, controlling and ignoring decay. We spray and otherwise treat foods to inhibit it. We have frequent garbage pick-ups to remove decay, and we send our refuse to out-of-sight landfills so it can rot elsewhere.

At the same time as we are throwing away garbage, we are also depriving the land of valuable materials. All that rotting, natural stuff is not only good for the soil, it's essential to soil health and plant growth. We may go to great lengths to bag up dead leaves and garden cuttings in the autumn, only to have to buy new topsoil and fertilizers in the spring.

Even the word rot itself sounds unpleasant, as do the other words that describe a perfectly natural and necessary process: decay, breakdown, putrefaction, spoilage. . . .

Maybe this explains why some people view compost heaps with more than a small measure of suspicion. Compost is the place where the rotting, the decay that we'd rather keep out of sight, occurs.

Well, there is something happening to the cultural currency of composting. Composting has become "eco-chic" — no backyard is complete without a heap, people talk about composting at parties, neighbours compare composting stories, people have opinions about composting.

What has caused this cultural swing? (After all, many of our grandparents had compost piles in their backyards — composting was just something most households did.) Perhaps as a society we are recognizing that our wasteful ways are contaminating, polluting, harming and otherwise destroying the earth. The current garbage crisis is just one symptom of our throw-away system, a system based on consumption, on more of everything. But we're starting to recognize that there are limits to growth, that uncontrolled growth is the modus operandi of the cancer cell.

By composting — in our backyards, on our balconies, even in our basements — each one of us can do something to alleviate the burden of our wasteful habits. Composting is one small, positive step that we can all take to help the environment. And it's a great way to give back nutrients to the soil, to participate in the natural cycle of growth and decay and growth again. As Stevie Daniels in *Organic Gardening* (February, 1990) sees it: "When you put kitchen and yard waste in a compost pile you create the richest soil amendment available. You see the result of your action. . . . Our future depends on partnership, on our ability to cooperate just as the sun, air, water, plants and soil do, to ensure a healthy habitat for all. We see that partnership in our gardens and we begin to express it in all areas of our lives."

THE BIGGER GARBAGE PICTURE
Garbage is something that we used to be able to forget — aside from the small inconvenience of taking it out to the curb, tossing it down the chute, carting it to the dump, or burning it in the back field. Our garbage has become more than an eyesore — it's turned into a "crisis." Quite simply, we produce too much of the stuff.

For example, if you were to save all the garbage that you throw away in a year, you would have a pile that weighed about 730 kilograms (1,500 pounds). Estimates vary, but each American throws out, on average, 2 kilograms (4.3

pounds) of garbage every day; each Canadian, on average, throws out 1.7 kilograms per day. And we're running out of options for dealing with garbage. Unless it's stored in state-of-the-art facilities, landfills produce toxic runoffs and gases, incineration can produce toxic emissions, and more and more communities are saying "not in our backyards" to landfill sites.

Add to this the growing number of laws that ban certain materials such as lawn clippings and yard waste from garbage collection, and we indeed have a crisis. At present, a growing number of American states along with a number of Canadian municipalities have legislated some kind of ban or restriction on leaves, grass and/or yard waste in landfill, and we can expect more and more communities to follow their lead. This provides quite a strong incentive to start looking at alternatives such as composting.

The 3 Rs: Reduce, Reuse, Recycle
The "3 Rs" have become the rallying cry for garbage reduction, and composting fits into each of the Rs. By composting, you reduce the amount of garbage you throw out, you reuse materials, and you recycle nutrients back into the soil.

Before you throw anything away, ask yourself, "Is one use enough?"

The 25 Percent Solution
If we're running out of places for waste, then it helps to look at the composition of that waste. A high percentage of our "garbage" isn't really garbage at all. Rather, it is recyclable, reusable material that we could make use of in a much more efficient way. The Environmental Protection Agency (EPA) estimates that almost 18% of municipal solid waste is yard trimmings and almost 7% is food waste. According to the Earthworks Group, Americans throw away 24 million tons of leaves and grass every year. In Canada, the figures are equally startling: according to Environment Canada, ap-

proximately 25 percent of the garbage in municipal landfill sites is organic household waste that could be composted.

WHAT'S IN WASTE
United States

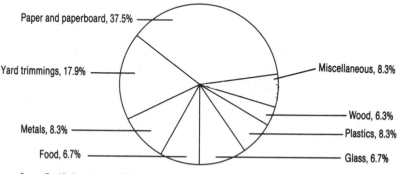

Paper and paperboard, 37.5%

Yard trimmings, 17.9%

Metals, 8.3%

Food, 6.7%

Miscellaneous, 8.3%

Wood, 6.3%

Plastics, 8.3%

Glass, 6.7%

Source: Franklin Associates Ltd. (1986)

Canada

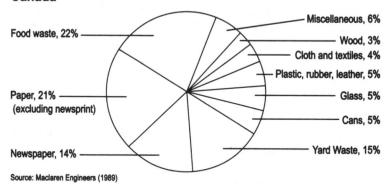

Food waste, 22%

Paper, 21%
(excluding newsprint)

Newspaper, 14%

Miscellaneous, 6%

Wood, 3%

Cloth and textiles, 4%

Plastic, rubber, leather, 5%

Glass, 5%

Cans, 5%

Yard Waste, 15%

Source: Maclaren Engineers (1989)

Thus, at least 25 percent of our "garbage" is compostable matter — materials that in nature never make a one-way trip to landfill but are endlessly recycled back into the soil. As Catherine Foster writes in *The Organic Gardener*, "In the process of nature there is no throwing away."

SOIL BENEFITS

Garbage reduction, however, is just one side of the composting coin. Compost also "feeds" the soil, providing the organic matter and nutrients necessary for growing things. Around the world, soil is rapidly being depleted and destroyed by our agricultural practices — we have to think of the soil under our feet as a threatened and endangered ecosystem.

According to the Worldwatch Institute, an estimated 25 billion tons of topsoil are lost from croplands worldwide every year. Along with the many other strategies, composting is one way to return fertility to the earth, to help repair a damaged environment.

Although we may think of the earth's elements as infinite, they are not. As we learned in high-school science, matter is neither created nor destroyed. It is, instead, cycled and recycled, transformed and moved across the globe. We breathe atoms that have been around for centuries; we drink water that has been through countless rivers; we eat from soil elements that were once part of a living plant. Nature is cyclical. Plants grow, die and decay — their nutrients are returned to the soil where they feed other living plants.

This is the true value of composting. Not only does composting reduce our garbage production by approximately 25 percent, it also returns nutrients and beneficial organisms to the soil. This is the soil that, along with air and water, provides the basis of life. So, by composting, we are putting ourselves back into the cycle, the cycle of nature, the cycle of life — a cycle on which the health of the planet depends.

▪ 1 ▪

Life in the Compost Heap

The principle involved [in composting] is really nothing
more than the law of good housekeeping, or good
earthkeeping — when you're finished with something,
put it back where it belongs!
— Steve Smyser, *Organic Gardening*

Composting* is as old as the soil itself. It's nature's way of
recycling nutrients and organic matter back into the soil
for use by new and growing plants. In this cycle, nothing is
wasted. Dead materials actually feed living matter.

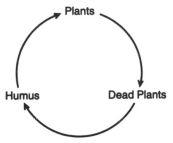

The Compost Cycle: Plants grow. Plants die. Dead plants turn into humus, which
provides nutrients for soil in which plants will grow.

When plants die and fall to the forest floor, micro-
organisms feed on them, breaking them down into smaller
and smaller components. When fully decomposed, the

*Terms shown in the text in boldface type are explained in the Glossary.

1

material is called humus, and it is full of the nutrients contained in the original plants. Thus, the nutrients are
returned to the soil, available for the living plants, and soil
fertility is maintained.

WHAT IS COMPOSTING?

In nature, the process of decomposition can take a long
time. Composting, though, speeds this process — providing
ideal conditions so decomposition can take place faster.

By digging, turning, layering and watering, you may feel
as if *you've* done the composting, but the work is actually
done by **decomposer organisms**, which form a lively, teem-
ing community in your heap. The process is started by bacteria and fungi, which break down organic matter for their
own food. (If you're wondering where the bacteria come
from, they arrive in the heap by the millions, attached to
every piece of organic matter that is put in the pile.)
Bacteria and fungi immediately get to work on organic
matter, breaking down the tissue, using its carbon for their
source of energy (so they can keep on eating), and using
the nitrogen to build protein in their bodies (so they can
keep on growing and reproducing). It's a simple life, but a
short one.

To say that bacteria are prolific is an understatement —
the rate at which they can reproduce is the stuff of horror
movies: "It has been calculated that if a single bacterium
divided every hour and every subsequent bacterium did the
same, 17 million cells would be produced in a day. A mass
the size of the earth would be produced in six days."
(Henry D. Foth, *Fundamentals of Soil Science.*) Of course,
such out-of-control growth assumes ideal conditions, conditions which, happily for us, are never met!

The population of bacteria in a compost community is
constantly changing. In addition, higher or more complex
forms of organisms work with bacteria. As well, when
bacteria die, they become food for other organisms.

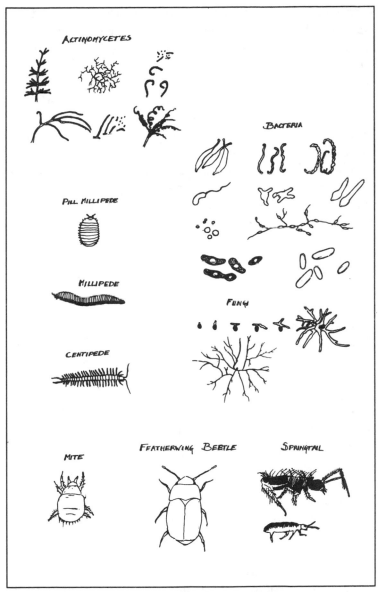

A few of the many creatures that live in a compost pile. (Not to scale.)

Actinomycetes, a higher form of organism that produces geosmin, the substance that gives soil its earthy smell, join the decomposition cycle, as do protozoa (single-celled, the simplest form of animal) and fungi. Larger decomposer organisms that you can actually see in your heap include mites, millipedes, centipedes, sow bugs, springtails and earthworms. Some of these larger decomposers chew their way through materials, breaking them up into smaller pieces that micro-organisms then feed on.

The final product of all this decomposition activity is called **humus** — a dark, sweet-smelling, soil-like material that is full of nutrients. Humus is a soil conditioner. That is, it improves the soil by holding moisture so plant roots have a water source during times of drought, and by holding and slowly releasing nutrients (like nitrogen, phosphorus) and **trace elements** (like zinc, boron, iodine) so that these are available for plants to take up through their roots.

STAGES IN THE LIFE OF A PILE

The food chain in a compost pile is remarkably elegant. Bacteria and other life forms break down materials into simpler forms for other bacteria and organisms to consume. Although there are many different types of bacteria in a compost pile, the population does shift and change in cycles as the environment in the pile changes. As bacteria break down materials into simpler forms, heat is produced. The more bacteria there are working, the hotter the heap gets. As the temperature rises, the bacteria producing the heat die off. They have literally created a hostile environment for themselves; but they have created a home for another set of bacteria that thrives in hotter temperatures.

Bacteria that work in the lowest temperatures are called **psychrophilic** bacteria. They are most active around 13° C (55° F) but they can also work at temperatures below freezing. These psychrophiles give off very little heat, but they do produce some, and along with a warming outside temperature, the heat in the heap builds to the point where another set of bacteria — **mesophilic** bacteria — start to take over. These mesophiles do most of the composting work. Their working temperature range is generally between 8° C and 50° C (46-120° F). As a byproduct of their activity, mesophiles produce acids, carbon dioxide and heat. However, because mesophiles can't survive in temperatures above 50° C, they begin to die off or move to the outer part of the heap. Again, they are so successful in their heat-producing work that they create an environment that is too hot for them.

Another type of bacteria called **thermophiles** then invades the heap, continuing the decomposition process. Thermophiles have been called the "hot shots" of the compost heap because they work at temperatures of approximately 50-90° C (120-194° F). They will keep decomposing material until either it gets too hot for them or they've used up too much of the degradable materials to sustain their population (eaten themselves out of a home!). So the temperature of the pile decreases.

As the thermophiles die off, the heap moves into its maturation stage in which mesophilic and psychrophilic bacteria populations come back and consume any remaining organic material. If you add more organic material at this stage, or turn the pile to move outside material into the centre, the cycle of different bacterial stages will start again.

During the maturation stage, larger organisms such as earthworms and ants may be found in the heap. By the end of this stage, you have stable, finished humus — compost ready for the garden. And this finished compost is full of life, particularly micro-organisms that are good for the soil. According to Jennifer Bennett, "A single gram of wet, 158° F compost contains more than one billion bacteria and 10 million fungi." (*The Harrowsmith Reader III*)

HEAT IN THE HEAP

Reaching the thermophilic stage (the hottest part of the cycle) is desirable for composting, but achieving optimum conditions for these bacteria to grow and multiply demands some work. This stage is important because almost all pathogens in plant and animal materials and weed seeds are killed off at temperatures around 60° C (140° F), a temperature only reached in an "active" or thermophilic heap. (Of course, the possibility of pathogens in compost will be greatly reduced if no pet waste, diseased plants, manure from diseased animals, or meat and dairy products are used.) However, many casual backyard composters don't worry about reaching this optimum stage, and they still end up with fine, finished compost — it just takes them a bit longer.

FOOD FOR THOUGHT

Energy conservation enthusiasts may want to know more about the potential uses of the heat produced by active compost piles. Plans and information on a water preheater that uses the heat produced by decomposing leaves are available from Nature's Way. (See Sources.)

HAPPY AND HEALTHY MICRO-ORGANISMS

The needs of decomposer organisms are the same as those of any living thing: oxygen, food and water. Good composting provides these in the proper balance required by the decomposer organisms so that they can do their job efficiently. In other words, your role as compost "facilitator" is to provide an environment for fast decomposition — the proper balance of oxygen, food and water. If you follow the simple steps outlined in this book, you can't go wrong.

Air

To say that all bacteria require air is a bit misleading because there are in fact two types of bacteria: **aerobic,** which need oxygen, and **anaerobic**, which require an absence of oxygen.

Aerobic bacteria require oxygen in order to decompose organic material. When these bacteria digest materials, they give off energy in the form of heat. This heat is energy in excess of what the bacteria need. The temperature in the pile rises as the bacteria give off more and more heat, and as the heap gets hotter, the bacteria require more and more oxygen because they are working harder.

You can create a composting environment for anaerobic bacteria (see "Anaerobic Composting" in Chapter 2), but this process is incredibly smelly. As well, high temperatures are not reached in anaerobic composting, and thus any pathogens or weed seeds present in the compost materials are more likely to survive. Therefore, most backyard composters want to encourage aerobic conditions in their heaps.

COMPOSTING PROCESS

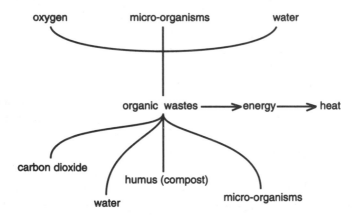

Organic wastes are the basic composting materials. The micro-organisms that live on organic wastes, or that are introduced to the waste through the soil, break down the waste, but they need oxygen and water to do so. During this process, the micro-organisms give off excess energy in the form of heat. When the micro-organisms have fully broken down the organic matter into its simplest components, the end result is humus or compost, which is full of micro-organisms, carbon dioxide and water.

Food

Bacteria are voracious and they are also incredibly adaptable. Most can produce the proper enzyme to digest whatever materials they encounter, but they break down different materials at different speeds. Their only requirement is that their food be organic — something that is, or once was, alive.

All living things contain carbon and nitrogen. Bacteria feed on carbon, which they get from carbohydrates, and nitrogen, which they get from proteins.

The greater the variety of materials you feed the microorganisms in the heap, the greater the variety of nutrients in your finished compost.

Water

To function properly, decomposer organisms need water. A heap that has less than 40 percent moisture content will work very slowly, but if a heap has over 60 percent moisture, the aerobic bacteria will drown and smelly anaerobes will take over. Because it's difficult for the backyard composter to measure the exact moisture content of the heap, the general rule is that the heap should be as moist as a wrung-out sponge.

Although this chapter outlines the general processes and cycles that occur in composting, it's important to remember that aside from the basic principles, every compost pile is different. It's not necessary to memorize all the scientific terms. Rather, it's only important to find a method that works for you — and if you can do this without knowing a mite from a mesophile, then just keep on composting.

HEAPS IN HISTORY

"One acre composted is worth acres three
At harvest thy barns shall declare it to thee"
— Thomas Tusser, 1557

Composting has been going on for as long as there has been soil, and long before humans labelled it.

Ancient Greeks had a word for it; the Talmud describes it; the Bible mentions it.

Even George Washington experimented with compost. In his diary entry of April 14, 1760, Washington recorded an experiment that he carried out on his rows of growing wheat. Needless to say, the wheat planted in compost and sheep dung grew best, he concluded.

The soil advice provided by James Madison, the fourth president of the United States, is as good today as it was in 1818, when he said to the Agricultural Society of Albemarle, Virginia: "The most logical mode of preserving the richness and of enriching a farm is certainly that of applying a sufficiency of manure and vegetable matter in a decomposed state."

■ 2 ■

Compost Methods: The Fine Art of Decay

For me, compost will forever be the real garden magic.
Live food for live plants, forever renewing the earth,
improving its structure, correcting both acid and lime
conditions, mulching out weeds — and it's free. I swore
I would never be without it again, and I never have.
— Midge Ellis Keeble, *Tottering in My Garden*

People often ask, "Well if anything organic eventually
decomposes, why bother with a compost heap? Why not just
throw all raw waste into the soil and avoid the work of
organizing and maintaining a pile?"

If you put raw wastes directly into the soil, the decomposition process will rob the soil of nitrogen, an important
nutrient for plants. (But see "Soil Incorporation" later in
this chapter for a method of composting this way.) Finished
compost from a pile is usually a superior, balanced product.
This is because of the combination of materials that you put
in a pile, the balancing of carbon and nitrogen materials
that is difficult to achieve from just random dumping. Since
one of the benefits of composting is that you're enriching the
soil, it's better to encourage the building of soil nutrients
rather than depleting them.

In a controlled compost environment, you can also take
steps to ensure the high temperatures needed to kill weed
seeds, diseased plant tissue and pathogenic organisms, some-

thing that you won't achieve if you just throw waste onto the soil.

And finally, while it is true that all living things eventually break down, you can avoid potential problems with odour, pests and slow decomposition in the controlled environment of a compost pile.

You can make compost above the ground in bins, boxes, garbage cans, bags, barrels or piles.

You can make compost on the ground in rows.

You can make compost below ground in pits, trenches or holes.

You can make compost inside, outside, on a balcony, a deck or in a garage.

CHOOSING A METHOD

How you compost depends very much on your own needs and situation: how much space you have available, what materials you have, what you want the compost for, how much time you want to spend, how tidy you want your compost pile to look, etc. If, for example, you want to produce a little compost with minimum effort in a small area, then your best choice might be a commercially available container or bin. But, if you have a lot of space and want as much finished compost as possible, you may want to build a deluxe three-bin unit.

(If you ever need composting inspiration, just think of the Seattle zoo's composting program. They convert over 500 tons of animal wastes and landscape clippings into 1,000 cubic yards of "Zoo Doo" every year! Now think of your backyard or balcony — small potatoes, small problems!)

Composting systems vary greatly — from a simple bin to piles that require weekly attention. Some systems use containers; others don't. Some can be used indoors; most are for outdoor use. However, all systems fall into one of the following categories: 1) holding units; 2) turning units; 3) mulching; 4) soil incorporation; 5) anaerobic composting; 6) worm composting; 7) cover crops or green manuring.

Holding Units

This is one of the easiest ways to compost and the most popular. Holding units for yard and kitchen wastes are usually enclosed in some way and contain these materials while they break down. (The commercial one-bin systems that are sold in gardening centres are holding units.)

Holding units may be enclosed by material such as snowfencing or concrete blocks. This type of enclosure makes it difficult to "turn over" the heap as a way of getting oxygen in, so holding units usually need (or at least benefit from) some kind of air stack or regular hole poking. While air stacks or poking means less work for you, in general it does take longer (than turning a pile) to produce finished compost — typically, six months to a year.

If you have room, it is a good idea to have two of these units: one that's full of maturing materials and another to which you add fresh waste. When the maturing heap is ready, you can put the compost in the garden and then start using that bin for fresh wastes, leaving the other to mature.

Advantages:

- You can add food and yard scraps continually to holding units, rather than waiting until you have enough materials to "build" a larger pile.
- Holding units need relatively little maintenance.
- Apartment dwellers can use them for composting on their balconies.

Disadvantages:

- Because you're not fully turning materials in a holding unit, it can take longer to produce finished compost.
- Finished compost will be at the bottom of the pile.

- Depending on what kind of holding unit you use, getting access to the compost may be difficult.

Detailed plans for building your own holding unit and descriptions of commercially available holding units appear in Chapter 3.

Turning Units

Turning units are compost systems that are designed to be turned or **aerated** (adding oxygen for faster decomposition). These systems work faster because oxygen encourages bacteria, and turning, if done properly, ensures that all materials get to the hot centre of the heap. There are many kinds of turning units: barrel composters; single units that come apart easily, are then re-assembled in another place and filled with the partly decomposed material; or two- or three-unit systems.

Turning units tend to work faster than holding systems. With a rotating composter (often a drum or barrel), you can get finished compost in as little as three weeks. In any turning unit, the speed of decomposition depends on how often you turn materials. (Even with a casual turning schedule, you will get finished compost in approximately three months.)

With careful monitoring of a three-bin unit (turning the heap when it has reached the optimum temperature), you can get finished compost in just a month or so.

Advantages:
- Turning compost materials promotes faster decomposition.
- Materials on the outside of the pile get moved to the hot inside, promoting thermal kill of weed seeds.

Disadvantages:
- Turning does require some work.
- Turning may be difficult for people with back problems or for gardeners "of a certain age."

Detailed plans for building your own turning unit and

descriptions of commercially available turning units appear in Chapter 3.

Mulching: Nature's Recycling

Mulching is, quite simply, composting slowly by adding a layer of organic insulation to the soil. This is what happens on the forest floor. When leaves fall off trees or plants die, they form a layer of mulch that slowly decomposes and eventually turns into humus. Nutrients in the humus are slowly released into the soil for use by growing plants.

Not only does mulching return organic matter, soil organisms and nutrients to the soil, but it also provides other benefits: it prevents weeds from growing (gardeners who practise mulching rarely need to pick many weeds), preserves moisture in the soil, keeps soil temperature constant, prevents wind erosion and keeps soil from compacting.

Mulching is often used by gardeners, not as a replacement for regular composting but as an adjunct or useful companion. If your main motivation for composting is to get rid of food waste and reduce the amount of garbage you throw out, mulching is a somewhat cumbersome and messy method. If, on the other hand, you're composting primarily to improve your garden soil, mulching is a great way to increase soil productivity.

Mulching is extremely simple. You just spread the organic mulching material on top of the soil, around plants or on top of garden paths. Garden mulch favourites include leaves, straw, wood chips (not sawdust), black-and-white newspaper, dried grass clippings, and composted manure. Food wastes should be used only with other mulching materials, dug into the soil, then covered with mulch.

Compact chipper/shredders can deal with large amounts of dead leaves and branches, turning them into good mulching materials. A few neighbours might get together to share the cost of this gardening tool. Check the Yellow Pages for companies that rent shredders and chippers.

In this example of mulching, compost has been used as a mulch around a tree, out to its drip line. Be careful not to pile compost against the trunks of trees or shrubs.

Your city or town may be able to provide you with mulching material (such as wood chips) at no cost. Contact your local parks department or the department that handles wastes.

Mulch can be spread on top of the garden in the fall. It will partially decompose over the winter and then can be dug into the garden in the spring or put into your compost pile. Or, mulching can be done around planting time in the spring and left throughout the summer and winter, and dug in when preparing the beds the next spring. If you're using a woody material for mulch, you may want to provide a nitrogen source such as bloodmeal or mix in a nitrogen-rich mulch such as composted manure.

For lazy or busy gardeners, mulching is a great gardening shortcut. It reduces weeding dramatically, cuts down on the need for watering and protects the soil (and shallow plant roots) from the harsh mid-summer heat or winter cold. However, mulch can also harbour slugs and earwigs. Alas, foolproof and perfect gardening techniques still evade us.

Advantages:
• Mulching is a good way to utilize large amounts of leaves in the fall.
• Mulching is great for your garden and for the soil: it controls weeds, retains moisture in the soil, reduces rainfall runoff, prevents wind erosion, keeps soil from splattering onto plants during heavy rain, reduces soil compaction, and promotes the activity of soil organisms and earthworms.

Disadvantages:
• Food wastes, even if put underneath another mulching material, may attract pests such as raccoons.

Soil Incorporation

Also known as pit or trench composting, **soil incorporation** basically means burying your waste. It is a relatively simple way to compost, and with this method you're making the compost right where you use it — in the garden rows. It may be more appropriate if you have a large garden, because you don't plant in the places where you dig in your waste (for that year). As well, soil incorporation uses anaerobic bacteria, so it's slower than other methods, but since it works underground, you shouldn't have odour problems.

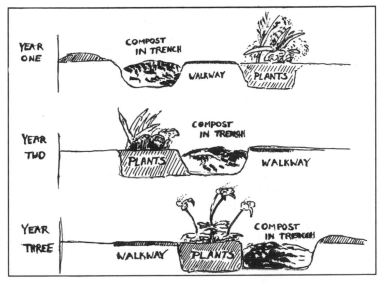

Compost is incorporated into the soil, covered with dirt and left to decompose in the soil.

In pit or trench composting, you dig holes or a trench row (approximately 15-18 inches deep) in your garden. You can put food waste, dead leaves and garden clippings into the hole, and then it is important to cover materials with at least four inches of soil. When the trench is full, leave it for three to six months. The smaller the pieces you put in, the faster the decomposition. Don't plant anything on top of the trench until all of the materials have decomposed.

You can set up a rotation for trenches to get the most out of the finished compost. For example, organize your garden around a three-row system and a three-year rotation. The first row is for making compost; the second row is planted; the third row is a path. In the next year's planting season, the first row becomes the planting row; the second row becomes the path; the third row becomes the new trench for composting. If you continue this cycle, you'll always be planting in fertile compost beds.

Advantages:
- You're making compost right where you use it.
- Compost-making is out of sight — buried.

Disadvantages:
- Some buried food waste may attract animals.
- A trench or pit requires some energetic digging.
- The garden space used in pit or trench composting is out of commission until the wastes have decomposed.

Anaerobic Composting

The bacteria that work in this method are called anaerobes — they work only in the absence of oxygen. So, you need a completely enclosed system and you can't keep adding wastes. Instead, you have to save up food and garden scraps until you have enough to fill about half a large garbage bag. As long as the bag is kept airtight, there's no odour — until you open the bag!

To make compost, just fill a sturdy garbage bag approximately one-third with soil. Use food scraps for the next third, and make the final third of dead leaves or garden clippings. Water the contents until damp but not soggy. Tie the bag so that no air can get in. (For extra strength, place the bag inside another garbage bag.) Roll it around to mix materials, and place in a sunny corner. If you roll the bag about once a week, you should have finished compost in about six weeks.

Be forewarned: when you open the bag to harvest your compost, there may be some odour. Also, be sure to reuse the bag.

Advantages:
- This is a low-maintenance, minimum-attention method of composting.
- It can be done on an apartment balcony.

Disadvantages:
- You can't keep adding food waste to the bag. You need to save materials and fill the bag all at once.

- You will need a few bags on the go at once if you produce a lot of food and garden wastes.

Note: It is possible to compost anaerobically using a *sealed* composter.

Worm Composting

Vermicomposting is composting with worms — they do most of the decomposition work. In colder climates, worm composting is done indoors, though you can put the worm bin outside in the summer. You need special worms, not the regular "garden-variety" earthworms, which will die in a worm bin. Worm composting produces nutrient-rich worm castings as well as humus. It's an ideal composting method for people who live in apartments and want to reduce their garbage output.

Since this method of composting is so distinct, we have devoted an entire chapter to the subject (see Chapter 9).

Advantages:
- Ideal for apartment dwellers.
- Very popular with kids.
- Quite a conversation piece.
- Vermicomposting is a good way to compost food wastes if your regular outside pile attracts pests.

Disadvantages:
- Can't handle grass clippings or yard wastes.
- Some people are squeamish about worms.
- You have to be careful about fruit fly infestations.

Cover Crops and Green Manures

The growing of cover crops (also called the practice of green manuring) combines the principles used in both composting and mulching. Cover crops are fast-growing, usually nitrogen-fixing, plants such as clover that are grown specifically to be ploughed under before maturity, to enrich the soil. While these plants are growing, they act as "living mulch."

When they are turned under the soil (before they have gone to seed), they decompose and their nitrogen and organic matter enrich the soil.

The practice of growing cover crops is called green manuring — you are fertilizing the soil with manure, albeit plant or green manure. (You can also think of green manuring as "growing" good soil.) Green manuring is done at different times in the growing season, depending on the climate, the type of cover crop, and the other crops being grown.

Basically, cover crops such as alfalfa, rye, sweet clover or vetch are planted for the purpose of being ploughed under — they grow quickly and once turned under, they return their goodness to the soil. By the time you're ready to plant a flower or vegetable crop in that spot again, soil microorganisms will have decomposed all the cover crop material, releasing nitrogen into the soil and increasing its organic matter content.

Before digging in the cover crop, you may want to cut it first, allow it to dry out a bit, and then turn the whole crop under the soil. To get the most benefit, don't dig the green material in too deep, a few inches is fine. For those of you who are already composting, you'll recognize that green manuring or the planting of cover crops is basically just composting quickly in the soil, rather than in a compost bin.

Green manuring is an incredibly versatile gardening practice that can be done at many different times: a fast-growing cover crop may be planted in the late summer or early fall, to be ploughed under in the early spring, approximately four to six weeks before transplanting seedlings. If winters are not severe in your area, a cover crop can be started in late fall. These two timings have the added advantage of keeping the soil "covered" over the winter and preventing erosion.

Or, you can plant a fast-growing cover crop in the early spring, turning it under a few weeks before planting your vegetables. Avid gardeners will also take advantage of any bare patches in the garden — after early crops (such as radishes) have been harvested — by planting a cover crop. If you have severely depleted soils, you may want to devote a whole growing season to a cover crop, cutting and turning it before it goes to seed, thereby returning fertility to the soil.

Advantages:

- Holds soil in place, prevents erosion.
- Adds nutrients to the soil when turned under.
- Improves soil structure by increasing aeration and drainage in the soil.
- Crowds out and discourages weeds.
- Attracts beneficial insects.

Disadvantages:

- The garden space you plant with cover crops will be out of commission for the duration of the cover crop's growth.
- Digging the cover crop into the soil requires hard work.
- This composting method will not utilize your food waste and garden clippings.

SOME COMMON COVER CROPS

Annual rye-grass: plant in spring, turn under before it blooms in mild areas; or plant in fall for spring turning.

Barley: plant in spring, turn under before blooming; or plant in fall for spring turning (will tolerate cold winter).

Winter wheat: plant in fall for turning under in spring (will tolerate cold winter).

Alfalfa: plant in spring, turn under either before blooming or when in full bloom (will tolerate winter).

Crimson clover: plant in fall in mild areas for spring turning.

Dutch white clover: plant in spring or summer for pre-bloom turning (will tolerate winter).

Buckwheat: plant in spring or summer; turn over either pre-bloom or in full bloom.

CHOOSING A METHOD

Once you've considered the following questions, you will have a better idea of what system will work best for you.

- How much time do you want to devote to composting?
- How much labour do you want to devote?
- Do you mind turning the pile?
- How much space do you have for your composting unit?
- Do you have a lot of waste material or just a little?
- Do you have food scraps only?
- Do you have garden scraps only?
- Do you have a mix of materials?
- Do you want to compost grass clippings — or leave them on the lawn, which is much better for your grass?
- Do you want finished compost quickly?
- Do you want to construct your own bin or buy a bin?
- How much time do you want to spend constructing the bin?
- Do you want your bin to look like a "designer" bin?
- Do you anticipate having pests?

Of course, with all of this talk of bins, it's easy to forget that by far the oldest method of composting is a mound — a heap or a pile. This is also the cheapest method. Some people don't like the look of an unenclosed heap, but if you have the room, it's an easy way to make compost. Animals might be a problem, because there's no structure to keep them out of the compost, but if you're careful about covering food wastes, you may be able to avoid pests. However, if you live in an urban environment, unenclosed heaps are an open invitation to dogs, mice, raccoons and rats. If you're using an unenclosed heap, compost should be ready in about three or four months if you turn it once every few weeks. It will probably take a year if you just let it sit.

Variables	Methods	Holding Unit (e.g. drum or can, cinder block, snow fence)	Turning Units (Single) (e.g. barrel)	Turning Units (Double) (e.g. cinder block)	Turning Units (3 bin) (e.g. bin wooden)	Mulching	Soil (Pit or Trench) Incorporation	Commercial Bins	Worm Composting
Time	a lot				✓				
	medium		✓	✓	✓		✓		
	little	✓				✓		✓	✓
Labour	a lot			✓	✓				
	medium		✓	✓	✓		✓		
	little	✓				✓		✓	✓
Turning	required		✓	✓	✓				
	good idea	✓						✓	
	not necessary	✓				✓	✓	✓	✓
Space	a lot			✓	✓				
	medium		✓	✓					
	limited	✓				✓	✓	✓	✓
Materials	a lot		✓	✓	✓				
	medium	✓	✓	✓		✓	✓	✓	
	little								✓
Food Scraps	a lot		✓	✓	✓				
	medium	✓	✓	✓	✓		✓	✓	✓
	few					✓			
Garden Scraps	a lot		✓	✓	✓				
	medium	✓	✓	✓	✓	✓		✓	
	few						✓		✓
Speed	fast		✓	✓	✓				
	medium	✓	✓	✓	✓			✓	✓
	slow	✓				✓	✓		
Construction (make own)	cheaply	✓	✓	✓					✓
	quickly	✓	✓	✓					✓
	more elaborate			✓	✓	✓			✓
Bin Cost (buy)	inexpensive	✓	✓	✓				✓	✓
	medium cost	✓	✓	✓	✓			✓	✓
	"designer"	✓	✓	✓	✓			✓	✓
Pest Proofing	recommended	✓	✓	✓	✓		✓	✓	

*More than one check indicates that unit can be adapted to several requirements.

QUICK GUIDE TO BEST METHOD

Apartment dwellers:
- vermicomposting — composting indoors with worms
- composting in a garbage can with air stack on the balcony
- community composting outside as a group on apartment property
- rotating barrel or tumbler on balcony
- lined holding unit on balcony

House with little garden space:
- single-unit composting (can, drum, wooden box, commercial bin, snow-fence enclosure)
- vermicomposting

House with lots of outdoor space:
- 2- or 3-bin unit
- single units
- vermicomposting

■ 3 ■

To Build or to Buy?
Choosing the Right Bin

Basically, a compost bin is to soil building what a food
blender is to cooking: a time-saving innovation that
speeds up preparation.
— Ellen Cohen, *Organic Gardening* (July 1986)

There is probably no better measure of the astounding
increase in popularity of composting than the explosion of
choice in commercially available compost bins. From deluxe
models to build-your-own plans, there are bins for everyone.
Of course, not everyone needs a bin — many people make
compost quite happily with just a pile or mound in an out-
of-the-way corner of the garden. But for convenience, control and rodent resistance, commercial bins make an
attractive alternative to either an unenclosed pile or most
homemade bins.

In an urban backyard, commercial bins offer many advantages over simple compost mounds or heaps: you can produce finished compost in a smaller area because bins don't
take up much room; bins keep working-compost neat and
out of sight; and with a bit of pest-proofing, bins keep out
rodents. You can achieve the same results by building a compost enclosure, but there are many prefabricated, inexpen-
sive bins on the market to choose from, if you're not inclined
to construct your own.

The benefit of a compost bin, as opposed to a pile, is that it helps *you* make compost. Depending on how the bin is made, it may provide protection from the elements, keep the contents insulated, use solar energy to raise the temperature of the materials (and thereby extend the compost season) and help keep pests out. But a bin doesn't really change the decomposition process; it just makes your job easier and helps put *you* in control of the decomposition process.

In this chapter, we provide several plans for making your own compost bin and a guide to the variety of commercial bins available. It is not an exhaustive list, but rather a selection. You will probably find other bins for sale in your area, but they will most likely be variations of the types described below. Check with the manufacturer or retailer to find out whether the bin is guaranteed — many bins have a 10-year warranty. (Inclusion in this list does not imply any kind of endorsement.)

Before purchasing a bin, phone your local officials to see if your municipality is selling compost bins to home-owners and apartment dwellers at a reduced price. (If they're not, suggest that they might want to consider doing so.) Many communities are recognizing that subsidizing home composters is a great way to save landfill space and reduce garbage collection charges. Encourage your local officials to beautify every backyard with a bin!

MAKING YOUR OWN HOLDING UNIT
The following plans are for some common and relatively easy-to-make bins. You may want to experiment with some other scrap materials — just remember, bins should be at least three feet in each dimension for best results.

Mesh Holding Bin:
Materials:
- 13' of 1/2" hardware cloth
- 1-1/2' of heavy wire

Set-up:
- bend the hardware cloth into a circle, folding back 4" of the cloth at each end to provide a strong edge

- cut the heavy wire into ties using pliers, secure the two ends of the cloth with heavy-wire twist-ties in at least four places
- if you plan to put only leaves in the bin, you can just stand it upright; however, if you're adding heavier garden and food wastes, you should dig a shallow, round trench so the bin fits snugly in place

Use and Maintenance:

This bin is especially good for dead leaves and yard waste, and they can be added as they become available.

It may take as long as a year to make compost in this bin, although if you add waste continually, there may be some finished compost in the bottom of the bin earlier. You can either harvest the bottom material first (by lifting the unit to one side and digging it out) or wait until the bin is full and let it sit until all the waste has decomposed. To harvest a bin full of finished compost, just lift off the bin and scoop compost out.

Drum Holding Bin:
Materials:
- large metal drum or wooden barrel
- perforated pipe or tube for air stack
- a few cinder blocks or pieces of wood for the bin to sit on

Set-up:
- arrange cinder blocks or pieces of wood on the ground as a pedestal

- perforate the bottom of the drum or barrel in at least 10 places (approximately 1/2" holes)
- place drum or barrel on pedestal
- to keep air moving in this bin, you should put some kind of air stack or tube inside the bin. (See "Ventilation" in Chapter 5 for information about different materials you can use.)

Use and Maintenance:

This bin is best used for a mixture of food and garden scraps.

If you find that material becomes smelly, you may want to drill more holes in the sides of the bin for better aeration. As well, because adequate ventilation can be a problem in this bin, you should stir material regularly (about once a week) or poke holes in it with a stick.

To harvest finished compost, either dig down to the bottom, or wait until all materials have fully decomposed and empty the whole drum.

Garbage Can Holding Unit:
Materials:
- large garbage can with lid, made out of galvanized metal, aluminum or plastic

Set-up:
- drill approximately 35 holes, 1/2" diameter, all around the sides of the can
- drill several holes in the bottom as well

Use and Maintenance:
This bin may be used for food and yard wastes, though it won't hold a huge amount of garden wastes (think of how quickly garbage bags fill up with grass clippings).

Because of its relatively small size, it's a good idea to add a layer of sawdust or straw at the bottom of the can to absorb excess moisture and assist drainage.

Mix, poke holes with a stick, or stir the wastes once a week to keep odours down.

Add a thin layer of soil or dead leaves after each addition of food scraps.

To harvest finished compost, either dig down to the bottom (or tip the can over and re-fill the bin with the un-decomposed material), or wait until all materials have fully decomposed and empty the whole drum.

VARIATION FOR APARTMENT DWELLERS

If you have a porch or balcony, place the can on bricks, with a tray underneath.

You can drill fewer holes and put an air stack inside for aeration (plastic drainage tile with holes makes a good air stack or see Sources for commercially available air stacks).

Cinder Block Holding Unit:
Materials:
- approximately 48 cinder (concrete) blocks

Set-up:

- place four cinder blocks on each of three sides, build up four layers, leaving 3/4" air space between blocks. (Some people put the blocks on their sides, with the holes facing out.)

Use and Maintenance:

You can add food and yard waste to this bin, and its large size makes it particularly useful for dead leaves and grass clippings.

Since there's no lid, you should monitor the moisture level closely. Unless you're in an area that gets lots of rainfall, you'll probably have to add water to keep the moisture level like that of a squeezed-out sponge.

This type of heap gets a lot of air naturally, but stirring it occasionally will speed up decomposition, which can take up to a year in this kind of enclosure.

To harvest compost, dig from the bottom.

Note: This unit provides rodents with easy access.

Picket-Fence Holding Unit:
Materials:

- 12-1/2' of 3'-high snow-fencing or picket-fencing
- four corner posts, 3-1/2' high, made of wood or metal
- 48' of heavy wire

Set-up:

- clear a space about 3' square for your heap
- pound the four corner posts 6" into the ground, 3' apart, to form a square
- cut the heavy wire into three 16' pieces

- place the snow-fencing or picket-fencing around the posts on the outside, and use the wire to attach the fencing to the posts and the two ends of the fencing together, wrapping it at three different levels

Use and Maintenance:
Same as for Cinder Block Holding Unit.

Wooden Box Holding Unit:
Materials:
- 14' of 2"x4" untreated cedar (you can use any untreated scrap wood, but cedar is longlasting)
- five — 12' lengths 6"x3/4" untreated cedar
- galvanized nails

Set-up:
- cut the 14' length of 2x4 into four equal pieces for the corner posts
- pound them into the ground (down approximately 6" each, leaving them each about 3' high) in a 3' square

- cut each of the five — 12' lengths into pieces of 3' each to give you five boards for each side of the bin

- starting at the bottom, nail the boards to the corner posts, leaving air spaces of approximately 1/2" between each layer

Use and Maintenance:
Same as for Cinder Block Holding Unit.

Note: If you are using old wooden pallets to make this holding unit (as shown in the illustration), just nail the four sides together.

BUYING A COMMERCIAL HOLDING UNIT
Contact information for manufacturers of the holding units described below appears in the Sources section at the end of this book.

SoilSaver:

Manufactured by Barclay Recycling

Specifications:
- 12 cubic feet
- manufactured from recycled polyethylene
- lid that locks
- doors on the bottom of two sides for turning the compost materials and for removal of finished compost

Accepts:
- garden and yard wastes, including grass clippings and dead leaves
- kitchen scraps, but no meat, bones or fish

Note: The manufacturer's literature suggests that you turn the contents of the bin four or five times in a summer, by digging materials out of the bottom and putting them on top. If this seems like too much work, you can stir, poke, prod and mix materials thoroughly every week or so, and you'll get finished compost in anywhere from three to six months.

> ## RULE OF THUMB
>
> Holding units will work faster and there will be less chance of odour if you poke air holes in the compost and stir materials once a week or so. A broom handle jabbed down at regular intervals and stirred will aerate the pile.

Bio-Keg:

Manufactured by Composting Systems

Specifications:

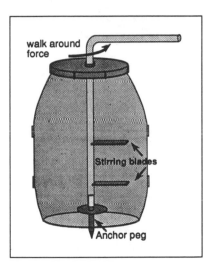

- made from re-used polyethylene plastic food barrel, approximately 3' high, 200-litre (45-gallon) capacity
- screw-on lid
- air enters through slots in the side
- open bottom

Accepts:

- kitchen waste, except meat and dairy products
- very small amounts of yard waste and grass clippings

Note: You can purchase an attachment called "The Mule," for stirring compost. (It's called "The Mule" because you walk around the compost bin, turning the handle.) To harvest finished compost, tip over the bin.

For energy conservationists: it's interesting to note that the manufacturers of the Bio-Keg use wind energy (two wind-powered turbines) to supply their manufacturing electricity needs.

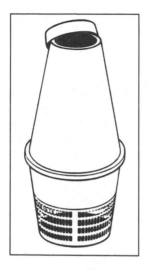

Green Cone:
Distributed by American Horticultural Society
Specifications:
- 14.73 cubic feet, polyethylene cone, 27" high
- lid
- cone sits on top of digestion chamber, which is buried in the ground
- no air holes, but inside vents for air circulation

Accepts:
- kitchen wastes, including meat, bones and dairy products
- very small amounts of yard waste

Note: This is called a digester/composter because its primary function is to divert waste rather than produce large amounts of finished compost. No turning or stirring required. It works best in sunny location. According to the manufacturer, the bin should be emptied once every two or three years.

Com-Post Aerator:
Manufactured by Environ-Mate
Specifications:
- sturdy, perforated aerator with two central openings which is designed to go inside a garbage can or bag

Accepts:
- kitchen scraps, except meat or bones
- amount of yard waste depends on size of garbage can or bag

Note: Basically a tool to aid aeration so that you can compost aerobically and without odour in a covered container. This can be used in many different kinds of compost systems. The holes in the pipe provide a pathway for air to diffuse into and out of composting mass inside the bag or can.

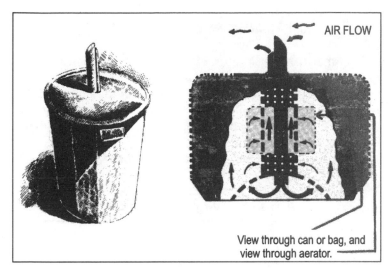

AIR FLOW

View through can or bag, and
view through aerator.

Wire Compost Bin:
Sold by Gardener's Supply Company
Specifications:
- 9- and 12-gauge steel with rust-proofing
- held together with corner rods
- holds 19 cubic feet of material

Accepts:
- kitchen waste
- large amounts of yard waste and garden clippings

AMERICAN HORTICULTURAL SOCIETY

The American Horticultural Society has put together a list of commercially available compost bins, which the AHS demonstrates at their National Home Composting Park in Alexandria, Virginia, and which they sell to the public by mail-order. For a copy of the list, send a business-size, self-addressed stamped envelope to
Compost Sources, American Horticultural Society
National Home Compost Park
7931 East Boulevard Drive
Alexandria, Virginia 22308-1300.

MAKING YOUR OWN TURNING UNIT
The following plans are for some relatively easy-to-construct turning units. You can also adapt holding units by doubling the bins, so that you turn the materials into the second bin.

Portable Wire Bin Turning Unit:
Reproduced by permission of the Seattle Engineering Department's Solid Waste Utility and the Seattle Tilth Association.
Materials:
- one 12' length of 2"x4" untreated cedar
- three 12' lengths of 2"x4" untreated fir
- 12' of 1/2" hardware cloth, 36" wide
- approximately 100 — 1-1/2" galvanized no. 8 wood screws
- four — 3" galvanized butt door hinges
- 150 poultry wire staples or a power stapler with 1" staples
- one tube exterior wood adhesive (10 oz)
- four large hook-and-eye gate latches

Set-up:
- cut each of the 12' 2x4s into four pieces 3' long. Cut a section 3/4" deep and 3-1/2" wide out of each end on the 4" side, for a total of 32 lap cuts.

- make four 3'-square frames from the lap-jointed 2x4s. Fill the gaps with exterior wood adhesive and fasten each joint with four screws.
- cut the hardware cloth into four 3'-square sections. Bend the edges back 1" for strength.
- centre each piece of hardware cloth on each of the four frames, pulling the cloth as taut

as possible, and fasten with wire staples.
- connect each pair of frames together with two hinges.
- put the hook-and-eye gate latches on the other ends of the frames so that the sections latch together.

Use and Maintenance:

To turn the compost, unhook the latches and lift the bin off the pile of composting materials. Re-assemble the bin close by and shovel all undecomposed materials into the new set-up, being careful to mix materials thoroughly. Remove any finished compost when turning.

Two- or Three-Bin Cinder Block Turning Unit:
Materials:
- approximately 100 cinder (concrete) blocks

Set-up:
- put 12 cinder blocks in a row, with approximately 1/2" between each block.
- put two rows of four cinder blocks, one row at each end, perpendicular to the long row.
- place two more rows of four blocks each on the ground inside the bin, at an equal distance from the two ends, dividing the bins into three sections.

- build up a second layer of blocks, staggering them for extra strength and leaving approximately 1/2" air space between each. Follow the same procedure for the third and fourth row.

Use and Maintenance:
Same as for Cinder Block Holding Unit, except materials are turned into second or third section for faster decomposition.

Note: This unit is not rodent-proof.

Wood and Wire Three-Bin Turning Unit:
Reproduced by permission of the Seattle Engineering Department's Solid Waste Utility and the Seattle Tilth Association.
Materials:
- two — 18' 2"x4"s
- four — 12' or eight — 6' 2"x4"s
- one — 9' and two — 6' 2"x2"s
- one — 16' 2"x6"

- nine — 6' 1"x6"s
- 22' of 1/2" hardware cloth, 36" wide
- 12 — 1/2" carriage bolts 4" long
- 12 washers and 12 nuts for carriage bolts
- three lbs of 3-1/2" galvanized nails
- 1/2 lb of 2-1/2" galvanized casement nails
- 250 poultry wire staples or power stapler with 1" staples
- one — 12' and one — 8' sheet 4-oz clear corrugated fibreglass
- three — 8' lengths of wiggle molding
- 40 gasketed aluminum nails for corrugated fibreglass roofing
- two — 3" zinc-plated hinges for lid
- eight flat 4" corner braces with screws
- four flat 3" T-braces with screws

Set-up:

Build Dividers: Cut two 31-1/2" and two 36" pieces from each 12' 2x4. Butt-end nail the four pieces to make a 35"x36" square. Repeat for the other three sections. Cut four 37"-long sections of hardware cloth, bend back edges 1". Stretch hardware cloth across each frame, check for squareness of the frame and staple screen tightly into place every 4" around edge.

Set Up Dividers: Set up dividers parallel to one another, 3' apart. Measure and mark centres for the two inside dividers. Cut four 9' pieces out of the two 18' 2x4 boards. Place two 9' baseboards on top of dividers and measure the position for the two inside dividers. Mark a centre line for each divider on the 9' 2x4. With each divider line up the centre lines and make the baseboard flush against the outer edge of the divider. Drill a 1/2" hole through each junction centred 1" in from the inside edge. Secure baseboards with carriage bolts, but do not tighten yet. Turn the unit right side up and repeat the process for the top 9' board. Use a carpenter's square or measure between the diagonally opposite corners, to make sure the bin is square, and tighten all bolts securely. Fasten a 9'-long piece of hardware cloth securely to the back side of the bin with staples every 4" around the frame.

Front Slats and Runners: Cut four 36"-long 2x6s for front slat runners. Rip-cut two of these boards to 2"x4-3/4" and nail them securely to the front of the outside dividers and baseboard, making them flush on top and at the outside edges. Save remainder of rip-cut boards for use as back runners. Centre the remaining full-width boards on the front of the inside dividers, flush with the top edge, and nail securely. To create back runners, cut the remaining 2x6 into a 34"-long piece and then rip-cut into four equal pieces, 1-1/2"x34". Nail back runner parallel to front runners on side of divider, leaving a 1" gap for slats. Cut all the 6'x1"x6" boards into slats 31-1/4" long.

Fibreglass Lid: Use the remaining 9' 2x4s for the back of the lid. Cut four 32-1/2" 2x2s and one 9' 2x2. Lay out into position in ground and check for squareness. Screw in corner braces and T-braces on bottom side of the frame. Centre lid frame, place brace side down on bin structure and attach with hinges. Cut wiggle molding to fit the front and back 9' sections of the lid frame. Pre-drill wiggle molding with 1/8" drill bit and nail with 2-1/2" casement nails. Cut fibreglass to fit flush with front and back edges. Overlay pieces at least one channel wide. Pre-drill fibreglass and wiggle molding for each nail hole. Nail on top of every third hump with gasketed nails.

BUYING A COMMERCIAL TURNING UNIT
A list of manufacturers of the commercially available units described in the following section is included in Sources.

Biostack Composter:
Manufactured by Smith & Hawken

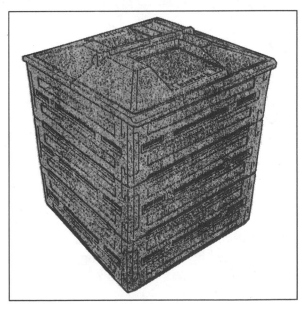

Specifications:
- three tiers that stack together
- lid

Accepts:
- kitchen scraps, except meat, bones and fish
- garden and yard waste

Note: You can add or subtract tiers depending on the size of your pile, but always keep lid on the top tier. The removable tiers make it very easy to turn and rebuild this kind of compost pile.

Garden Way E-Z Spin Composter:
Manufactured by Troy-Bilt Manufacturing Company

Specifications:
- large drum, rotating composter, with 9.6-bushel capacity
- comes with stand

Accepts:
- kitchen scraps except meat and bones
- yard waste

Note: Very easy to turn this kind of composter and if you turn regularly (once a day), can get finished compost in as little as two weeks. Because the drum is off the ground, this unit is virtually rodent-proof.

Enviro-Cycle:
Manufactured by Vision Recycling

Specifications:
- 6 cubic feet

- made from recycled plastic
- mounted on base

Accepts:
- kitchen waste including meat, bones and dairy
- yard and garden waste
  Note: Can be used on balcony or in garage.

BINS ON DISPLAY

If you're overwhelmed by the choice of bins on the market, you may want to ask neighbours and friends who are composting. They are an obvious source of information, but you can also try contacting a local environment or recycling group. As well, a few North American cities — Vancouver, Seattle and Toronto, for example — have "compost demonstration sites," where a variety of compost bins are on display. Often, these displays are staffed by composting experts who will answer your questions.

Multi-Bin Composting System:
Sold by Gardener's Supply Company U.S.
Specifications:
- two red cedar bins, slats for ventilation

- each bin holds 26 cubic feet
- sides held together with steel rods
- no lid

Accepts:
- kitchen waste
- large amounts of yard and garden waste

Note: To remove finished compost, lift out a corner rod and swing open as many slats from the bottom as necessary.

MAKING YOUR OWN UNENCLOSED TURNING HEAP
Fast Food: The 14-Day Compost Method

The following is a recipe for making quick compost. You don't need any kind of enclosure — instead, timed turning is the secret of this 14-day wonder. However, we've included this in the "make-your-own-bin" chapter because it is a lot of work — it's more like "building" a pile than just plain composting.

With this kind of compost system, you are building a hot heap; that is, a compost heap that reaches high temperatures to kill weed seeds and pathogens, and a heap that works in a short period of time.

To use this method, you must have all materials ready for composting at once; you don't add new scraps to the heap while it's working. But it works so quickly that you can save all your kitchen scraps for another heap at the end of 14 days. (When saving scraps, use a lidded container with layers of sawdust — avoid sawdust from treated or painted wood — or soil on top of each layer of food waste.) As well, you need to have enough room in your yard to be able to turn the heap into a new pile. This is the most labour-intensive method of making compost, but the reward is rich!

Bin or Heap:
You can make this fast compost either in an unenclosed heap or in a bin (commercial or homemade). The minimum size should be 3' x 3' x 3'.

Ingredients:
You'll need equal amounts (by weight is best, though you can also estimate by volume) of carbon-rich and nitrogen-rich materials (see Chapter 6). Start with a bottom layer of broken twigs or stalks or slightly compacted, shredded, dead leaves (approximately 4" thick), then add a 2" to 4" layer of grass clippings. Next comes a thin layer of food scraps (all shredded to 1" pieces). Continue adding layers to the heap, alternating the carbon materials (leaves, straw) with nitrogen materials (grass clippings, food scraps, manure). Keep the layers around 4" thick. You can also add a thin 1" to 2" layer of soil after the food scraps. If the materials seem dry, add water after each dry layer. Build to at least 3' high, but not higher than 5 or 6'.

Maintenance:
Your pile should heat up in the centre to about 130° F (55° C) after just three days (if it doesn't, you haven't added enough nitrogen-rich materials and you may want to remake the heap), at which point it is ready to be turned over. If you don't have a soil thermometer, then you won't be able to tell how hot the centre is, but you can still turn the pile after three days. If your pile is giving off a slight ammonia smell at

this time, this indicates that you've added too much nitrogen and the excess is lost to the air. Put a 1" to 2" layer of soil on top to trap the ammonia and thus conserve nitrogen in the pile.

After the first three days, turn the pile over (with a garden fork or shovel) into a new pile. Try to mix the materials completely so that the outer materials of the old heap are on the inside of the new heap. You'll still be able to recognize the different materials at this point. It's a good idea to chop through materials as much as possible when you're doing the turning.

Once you've turned everything into a new pile, wait another three days, then turn it all over into the original heap spot. Continue this process every three days. By the third turning, you probably won't be able to recognize the original materials. By the end of two weeks, you should have finished compost.

If you have a soil thermometer, you can test to see if the compost is finished. If it doesn't rise above 110° F (43° C) after the last turning (because the decomposer organisms have nothing more to work on), the compost is ready. You will have about half the amount of materials that you put on the original heap.

◼ 4 ◼

Calmposting:
Starting Your Pile

Answering the question, 'How should I make compost?' is rather like answering the question, 'How can I bake a cake?' It depends on what your objectives are, what materials and equipment you have to work with, and how much effort you are willing to put in.
— Stuart B. Hill, Ecological Agriculture Projects

The good news is that composting is a very forgiving process. Even if you start your pile in less than ideal conditions, the materials will eventually break down. However, the better your compost environment is in the first place, the faster the composting process will be, the better the final compost product will be, and the fewer problems you will have.

WHEN TO START? NOW!
If you don't have a bin or heap, now is the time to start, regardless of the season. Of course, the middle of a northern winter is not the most convenient of times, but you can put food scraps (which is probably about all you'll be adding in the winter) in the bin as you would in the summer, alternating layers with leaves saved in the fall. This is the only time of year when your garden soil is unavailable, so you may want to "kick start" the pile with some

47

commercially available compost accelerator (see "Activators, Starters, Inoculants" later in this chapter).

Bad news for procrastinators: you can start your compost any time in the spring, summer, fall, or even winter.

Autumn is a great time to start your pile because you'll probably have a good supply of dead leaves and garden scraps. (Save some leaves to add to the pile throughout the year.) But, of course, garden clippings are also in abundance in spring and summer, so you can start any time.

A Word About Winter

People often wonder what happens to compost in winter, what happens if a pile freezes, and whether or not it's okay to start a pile in winter and keep adding to it over the winter.

Decomposition slows down in winter. In very cold temperatures, it does stop. However, a compost pile in a protected area can be heated by the winter sun to become much warmer — sometimes even two to three planting-zones warmer than its immediate surroundings.

You should keep adding to the pile in winter, because the freeze/thaw cycle breaks down the cellular structure of materials. And when spring comes, the bacteria have a greater surface area to work on and the pile will heat up quickly, even if it has completely frozen in the winter.

One trick is to fill baskets with dead leaves in the fall, then keep them near your compost so you can cover up additions of food waste during the winter with this good insulating material.

If you start your heap in autumn and want to keep it as active as possible during the winter, you can add lots of nitrogen-rich materials and bulk up the heap with insulation. Layers of straw or leaves around the sides and on top will keep in some of the heat. These materials also provide a balance for the nitrogen-rich food scraps. You can also cover your heap in winter with an old carpet or plastic.

Although this will keep in the heat, it may also inhibit air movement and encourage anaerobic bacteria. You may want to experiment with this method and if your heap doesn't get too smelly, it's a great way to prolong the composting season.

If you harvest your compost in autumn and then dig a hole 6" to 12" deep underneath the bin, this will also keep some of the heat in when you're building up the new pile over the winter. Don't aerate your pile in winter unless odour is a problem, because turning or poking air holes in the pile will allow heat to escape.

WHERE TO START

Aside from a few considerations, where you put your bin is really a matter of personal preference.

Here are some important features for a choice location:

- Good drainage in the soil below the pile or bin.
- Protection from fierce winds.
- Ease of access for adding materials to the pile.
- Relatively level ground.
- Sun for most commerical bins.
- Shade for most wood and wire bins, which dry out.

It's best to put your pile in a sunny spot, but if your yard is completely shady, you can still make good compost. In fact, some people prefer a shady location — if their soil drainage is good, the shade keeps the pile from drying out. Conversely, if soil drainage is poor, you can put the pile in a sunny spot so it doesn't stay too moist. In full sun, there is the danger that the heap will dry out and you'll have to add water (in which case, you'll want the heap to be close to a water source). In a shady spot, of course, you won't be getting the benefit of the sun's heat, but the heap will heat up anyway if you're adding a good mix of materials. Whichever you choose, a level spot is best for drainage.

Some people avoid putting their piles too close to a tree because tree roots can "steal" nutrients from your pile. On the other hand, what's wrong with giving nutrients to a tree?

If you can, put the pile in a spot protected from high winds so materials won't blow off or be exposed to the wind-chill factor. Also, don't put the pile directly underneath downspouts or eavestroughs. Although this may seem like a convenient way to get water into the pile, you can't control excess water, which can lead to problems.

If this is your first compost bin, try to choose a permanent spot for the bin: it's a good idea to leave the bin in one place. The ground is full of decomposer organisms that migrate up into the pile. This is why it's best to have the pile on the earth, rather than on concrete slabs or pavement. Some people build heaps on slabs in order to prevent nutrients from leaching into the ground, or because they have no garden (apartment balcony, rooftop gardens, small city gardens). If you do this, you may want to put plastic underneath the bin to prevent the compost from staining the stone. However, plastic sheeting underneath can harbour flies.

Convenience is a big factor in deciding where you want your pile. Do you want your pile close to the house so you don't have far to take your food scraps or need to shovel a long path in winter? Do you want your bin close to the garden, both for ease of adding garden scraps and because the garden is where you'll use your finished compost? Wherever you decide to put your compost pile, it's important to leave room in front of the pile for ease of access.

You can even use the "companion planting" principle when finding a site for your heap. Worms love elderberry bushes (they find the leaves that fall very tasty), so if you plant this bush beside your pile or bin, you'll be encouraging a healthy worm population — great workers in your compost.

Some people "hide" compost piles in out-of-the-way places. Others don't mind having the bin in full view. One benefit of having it visible is that people may ask questions, providing you with an opportunity to learn new techniques or to educate others about the benefits of composting.

If possible, try to keep your bin away from your neighbours' outdoor entertaining areas. This way, if you do run into a problem with odour or flies, your compost won't cause offence while you're remedying the problem.

Yes In My Backyard!

According to the National Solid Waste Management Association in Washington, D.C., there are over 980 home-composting projects in operation in 31 states throughout the United States. In Canada, hundreds of municipalities are promoting composting and the number of programs will certainly increase as more and more communities ban yard waste from landfill sites. (Already, more than half of U.S. states have bans or restrictions on yard waste and grass clippings.)

The projects range from handing out subsidized compost bins to promoting composting at community workshops and demonstration sites. To find out if there is a compost project in your area — or to encourage your community to get involved — contact your community's waste management department, or your local recycling or environmental group.

RULE OF THUMB

The general rule is that your compost pile should be a minimum of 3'x3'x3'. The maximum size is around 5'x5'x5'. If you're using either a commercial or homemade bin, it is probably not as big as 3'x3'x3'. You can still make compost in a smaller enclosure. It's just that the ideal size for a heap is bigger.

SIZE OF PILE

If you are making an unenclosed compost pile, rather than using a bin, the size of the heap will affect the composting process. An unenclosed pile will work best if it is big enough to generate and hold heat, but not so big that air can't penetrate into the centre. However, like most things in composting, it's a matter of balance.

If you don't have enough materials when you start your pile to build it up to three feet high, it's okay. Just keep adding to the pile and eventually you'll build it up to a good height. When the pile is too small, it won't get hot enough to kill weed seeds or pathogens (though the chance that pathogens will be present is slight if you follow the guidelines on compost ingredients in Chapter 6). A small pile will still produce respectable compost — it just takes longer.

It may seem odd that a pile can be too big. However, if you build it higher than approximately five feet, the weight may compact the lower materials, preventing air circulation and causing anaerobic odours. If the pile is wider than approximately five feet, it's also difficult to achieve proper ventilation in the pile's centre.

RULE OF THUMB

If your compost pile is greater than 5'x5'x5' at the outset, push a ventilator tube through the middle of the pile to allow oxygen and moisture through. A ventilator tube can be a 2" plastic plumbing pipe drilled with 1/2" holes every 6" of tube length. Drainage tile tubing can give the same effect, mounted vertically in the centre of the pile.

Another consideration about volume is that the larger it is, the more work it is to turn it. So, if you have a lot of materials to start with, you may want to make two or more piles.

There are ways around the minimum and maximum sizes. Commercial bins, for example, are usually smaller and they still work. If you want a smaller heap, you can insulate the sides (with straw, for example). This will ensure hotter temperatures in the pile. If you want a larger heap, you can put **ventilation stacks** throughout the pile or turn it about once every three weeks. (For stacks, use perforated metal or plastic tubes, chicken wire wrapped in a circle, corn stalks, or bundles of twigs. They should stick out the top or sides of the heap.) These techniques ensure adequate ventilation.

Different materials can be used to provide adequate ventilation in a compost pile. On the left, weeping tile is used as an air stack; in the middle pile, both perforated plastic pipe and a bundle of twigs have been used; on the right, a commercial air stack is used to provide ventilation in a garbage-bag compost unit.

HOW? STARTING YOUR PILE

There are many different ways to set up your pile; each depends on what you want to achieve and what materials you have. You might review the compost methods discussed in Chapter 2, because the method you choose will affect how you set up your system.

Once you've chosen your composting method and the location for your pile or bin, you're ready to start adding material. It's a good idea to use a few shovelfuls of finished compost or soil as the bottom layer; this will be full of micro-organisms that will immediately get things "cooking." If you have any well-rotted cow or sheep manure, you can use it as a bottom layer — it's loaded with the micro-organisms that break down organic materials into compost.

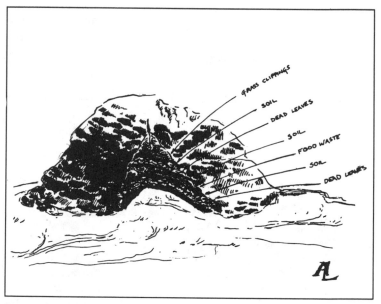

An unenclosed heap with materials added in layers.

Although you should start your heap with a mix of materials, it's not strictly necessary. A mixture will ensure faster decomposition, but if you only have food wastes and soil, you can still start a pile. (Try to scrounge some leaves or garden waste from neighbours.) Just start out with a layer of something bulky like dead leaves, if possible, and then layer food wastes with thin sprinklings (1") of soil.

To keep the bottom ventilated, you can put a layer of bulky yard waste such as hedge clippings as the first layer. However, this layer should not exceed 6".

If you have lots of material to start out with (dead leaves, garden scraps and food waste), then starting your pile is like "building" a layered cake. The goal is to alternate layers of **"green"** materials that are high in nitrogen (such as food scraps and grass clippings) with **"brown"** layers that are high in carbon (such as dead leaves). Each layer should be around 4" to 6" thick. For example, you can put one layer of dead leaves, then a layer of food waste, then a thin (1") layer of soil, then more dead leaves, a layer of grass clippings or manure, etc. You can also try to alternate wet and dry materials, so that the dry materials will absorb the moisture. (Wet materials tend to be "greens," dry materials "browns." For more information on "greens" and "browns," see Chapter 6.)

If all your materials are dry, you'll have to add water to each layer until the heap is as wet as a squeezed-out sponge. It's easier to add water to each layer rather than waiting until the pile is built.

It is best to start your pile with materials that have been well shredded (into 1" pieces) so that there is more surface area for micro-organisms to get working on.

If you find that you have too much material to start with (you must be the envy of every organic gardener around — all that composting opportunity!), and you suspect that the pile will get over 5' high, you can put stacks in the heap while you are building it, to ensure proper ventilation.

RULE OF THUMB

Organic material fed into your compost will decompose fastest when shredded into one-inch pieces, or smaller. A power lawn mower — set at its highest setting — is a terrific shredder for leaves, soft "greens" like spent tomato plants and annuals. Wear a pair of safety glasses and gloves. You can also put materials in a garbage can and shred them with a lawn edger.

Activators, Starters, Inoculants

These terms sound very scientific, but basically they include any materials that will stimulate or encourage decomposition in your heap. This is achieved in a number of ways: by providing micro-organisms that decompose organic materials, by adding nitrogen to the heap (nitrogen provides food for micro-organisms) and by altering the pH of the pile to encourage certain soil and micro-organism populations.

There are organic **activators** (manure, bloodmeal, compost or soil) and also artificial or synthetic activators (chemically synthesized compounds such as some commercial nitrogen fertilizers).

Conveniently, the best activators are finished compost and soil from your yard (store-bought soil is sometimes sterilized so it doesn't always add micro-organisms). A few shovelfuls of soil or compost will provide all kinds of micro-organisms. A thin layer after additions of food or garden waste works just fine. Of course, there are plenty of micro-organisms present in the food waste and garden clippings that you're putting on your heap.

A commercial compost **"starter"** or accelerator is a bit like fast food — you don't absolutely need it but it makes life easier. Accelerators help the decomposition process by adding nitrogen, enzymes and bacteria to the pile. If you're anxious about getting your pile working, you may want to experiment with accelerators, especially in winter when garden soil and compost are not easily available as natural activators.

As a nitrogen-source activator, you can use well-composted manure or bloodmeal. If you're using manure, it's better to let it dry out for a week or so, because fresh manure's high water content may prevent air from getting in to the heap. As well, manures that are very high in nitrogen ("hot" manures such as those from horses, sheep, poultry) may kill some micro-organisms, so let it rot first.

These natural sources of nitrogen are best because they also supply protein (which micro-organisms use), whereas chemical fertilizers do not.

Some commercial **"inoculants"** are available that claim to add special cultures of bacteria to your heap. These claims have not been backed up scientifically. Testing of artificial and organic activators have shown that ordinary soil from the yard is just as useful as commercial preparations. And it's free. As well, micro-organisms are already present in the materials you put on the compost

---

RULE OF THUMB

How much will compost compact from start to finish? Count on using three to five bushels of raw organic material for every bushel of finished compost you produce. (One bushel = eight gallons.)

If all of this advice has your head spinning, just follow the excellent suggestion for first-time composters: "Keep it simple; make it convenient; and keep yourself motivated until it's a habit." (The advice of Sharon Jones, a Toronto resident who helped motivate an entire neighbourhood into composting.)

■ 5 ■

Caring for Your Compost

Gardeners rave about it! Environmentalists sing its
praises! Politicians embrace it! What is it?
Decomposing organic matter!
— Henny Markus, *Green Living* (April-May 1991)

Defining the ideal compost process is as difficult as defining
the ideal tomato or cucumber. Is the ideal tomato one that
tastes the way tomatoes used to taste? Is it one that grows faster
and bigger than all others? Is it a tomato that resists pest infestations? Or is it a tomato that is hardy enough to survive the
transportation from farm to store? Although compost
aficionados tend to talk about compost perfection and ideal
conditions, there's no agreement about what that ideal is. For
example, you may not worry in the least if your pile takes two
years to produce finished compost. If your need for humus in
the garden is minimal, then someone else's ideal of producing
compost in just two weeks may be entirely inappropriate for
you. So, before you start comparing how your pile stacks up to
this nebulous idea of compost success, remember that your
needs and requirements are as individual as you are. Your goal
is to create a compost process that works for you.

There are a few themes that recur in compost talk, like:
don't worry if your pile isn't working perfectly, you can

adjust and experiment; or, everything will eventually decompose whether you provide ideal conditions or not; or, let your nose be your guide to how your heap is working; or, exact measurements of the carbon:nitrogen ratio, temperature and pH are not for everyone and you can compost without using anything even vaguely resembling a scientific instrument.

However, the message of this chapter is simply this: a little effort makes all the difference! By following a few guidelines and paying attention to a few signals from your pile, you will compost without odour, without animal intruders and without delay. And the finished compost will be great for your garden, full of nutrients and wonderful at improving the texture of your soil. So, what are these rules that help produce excellent compost?

- Feed your pile a balance of carbon and nitrogen materials, and chop them into small (1") pieces before adding to the heap.
- Aerate your heap so bacteria get oxygen to do their work.
- Provide enough moisture to keep the pile working.
- Provide "starter" bacteria (much as you would when making yogurt or sourdough bread) with some garden soil.
- Create a heap that is large enough to heat up but not so large that it compacts. (See Chapter 4 for more details on size.)

Each of these rules is covered in more detail later, but if you need a quick formula to remember the requirements of your heap, think of what *you* need: food, oxygen and moisture. It's the same for compost.

FEEDING YOUR PILE
There's more information on compost materials and the carbon:nitrogen ratio in Chapter 6, but one way to ensure good and fast composting, whether the materials are rich in carbon or nitrogen, is to chop them up into one-inch pieces. Think of the way that a big block of ice takes a

long time to melt, whereas cubes take less time and snowflakes disappear immediately. The principle is the same. Grinding, shredding or chopping the materials you add to your pile increases the amount of surface area on which micro-organisms can work. The bruises, punctures and tears also provide more places for the bacteria to invade the food (compare the tough protection offered by an apple peel to the fleshiness of the inside). By shredding material, you're breaking down the walls of the cell tissues, making the job of micro-organisms that much easier, and the composting that much faster.

Shredding into small pieces is great, but don't "powder" materials because they will compact and prevent air from circulating in the pile. If everything you put in the pile is the consistency of sawdust, you will have a gloopy mess.

Any chopper, knife, shredder, sharp spade or garden clipper will do. For garden wastes, some people use machetes. Some run their lawn mowers over dead leaves to shred them. (Set your mower at its highest setting and wear a pair of safety goggles.) If you have a lot of dead leaves and not a great deal of space for composting, but you want them to decompose quickly, you may want to get a special shredder attachment because it can be quite a strain on your mower's motor to run it over leaves. Or, you can use a lawn trimmer to shred leaves in a garbage can. (Be *sure* to wear safety glasses for this task.)

Another advantage of shredding is that you can mix materials right in the shredder. For example, adding equal weights of leaves and grass clippings and shredding them together will give you a good mix of carbon and nitrogen.

For kitchen wastes, you can use a sharp knife to chop materials. Some people use meat grinders to pulverize their compostable food scraps. Others use blenders to make "Garbage Soup": add food scraps and water and blend; pour over your heap. This can wear out the motor on the blender — and some people say it is inappropriate to use electricity to help make compost — but this method does speed decomposition.

FOOD FOR THOUGHT

The coffee grounds generated by the average office staff can amount to a significant volume. Why not take the grounds home with you? It will mean less garbage to deal with in the workplace (if you don't have an office worm composter), you'll have a good nitrogen source, and your colleagues may get interested enough in composting to start their own bins.

VENTILATION

Aerobic bacteria need air. If your pile isn't getting enough oxygen, then anaerobic bacteria will take over and the pile will start to smell — in fact, to reek! Words can barely describe the odour that's given off by a pile filled with anaerobes: rotten, foul, acrid, putrid just begin to describe the smell.

But if you keep a close check on the pile with your nose and follow a few simple aeration techniques, your pile should be fine.

- If you're putting a lot of very fine materials such as sawdust onto the pile, add fluffy materials such as straw to provide air passages, and then add some nitrogen-rich material to balance the carbon.
- Thick layers of dead leaves tend to mat. Therefore, it's best to put only thin layers of leaves (4" to 6") alternated with another material such as soil or food scraps.
- Fresh grass clippings also mat and turn into a slimy anaerobic mess. You can avoid this by putting on thin (4") layers and alternating these with material like leaves, to provide ventilation.
- A thin layer (3") of shrub or evergreen trimmings of a slightly woody nature allows oxygen between denser layers of material.

Getting Air In and Anaerobes Out

If you do absolutely nothing but put materials onto the pile and let it sit for a year, you will get finished compost. However, you may also get odour. Air penetrates only a few inches into the pile from the top, sides and bottom. To provide oxygen for the microbes in the centre of the pile and speed up the decomposition process, you have to get air in by turning, poking, stirring or jabbing. Of course, there's no hard and fast rule about aerating your heap: the oxygen requirements are related to a host of other factors such as moisture level, size of materials, texture and the original size of the pile. It's a juggling and balancing act. Experiment with different methods of aeration and you'll find what works best for you.

Turning

Turning is often discussed in terms of aeration; it's a great, if labour-intensive way to get air into your pile. Turning is also the way to get materials from the outer edges of the pile into the middle, so they will decompose and any potential pathogens on the outside of the pile will be moved to the hot centre. As an aeration method, turning makes sense only if you have either a two- or three-bin enclosed system or enough space beside an unenclosed pile to move your original pile from one place to another. If you have a commercial bin with doors at the bottom (e.g. a SoilSaver), then turning can be done by shovelling out the bottom layers and putting them on top. Or, to turn the contents thoroughly, you can completely disassemble the bin, put it back together in another place and turn the contents into the reconstructed bin. With some commercial bins, you may be able to lift the bin straight up and place it down in another spot, turning materials into the new place. For people whose backs are not up to strenuous tasks, aeration techniques of stirring or air stacking are discussed below. Or, try to encourage worms in your heap — dig them up from other places in the garden and put them in the heap. Worms do a great job of mixing materials but they will die off in a hot, active pile.

Turning compost is hard work. A cubic yard weighs approximately one ton! But turning does speed up

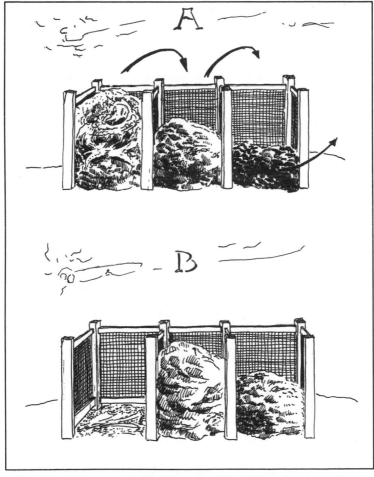

In illustration A, the compost in the right section of the bin is ready to be used on the garden. The decomposing material in the middle section can then be turned over into the right section of the bin and the material in the left section can be turned in the middle. You're then ready to start adding food and garden waste to the left section again (illustration B).

decomposition. Unless the pile starts to smell, casual composters can turn their piles every six weeks to three months. If the pile gets smelly, you can turn it every few days to get oxygen in; when it stops producing foul odours, you can revert to a more casual turning schedule.

Turning the pile too often (more than once a week) prevents micro-organisms from really heating up, because they are constantly regrouping after the disruption. If you are turning your pile regularly and things don't seem to be breaking down, overturning may be the problem (though this could be caused by a lack of nitrogen). You may want to let the pile sit for a few weeks and, if it's still not decomposing, add more nitrogen materials. Then you can go back to a regular turning schedule.

TEMPERATURE-BASED TURNING

For the serious composter equipped with a soil or compost thermometer, the compost temperature will tell you the best time to turn your pile. If you're careful about balancing the carbon:nitrogen ratio and you've chopped up materials, the pile should heat up to around 150° F (65° C) about four days after you've built the pile. (Of course, if you're building gradually, then your pile probably won't heat up until it's at least 3 feet cubed.) Turn the pile when it reaches about 150° F (65° C) and keep monitoring the temperature until it builds up again. When it does, repeat the turning process. With such fine-tuned turning, you should get finished compost in about six weeks.

Compost thermometers — with long stems — are available from many garden centres or by mail order from garden supply companies (see Sources).

If you don't need a precise reading but are just curious about the temperature in your compost pile, you can put a piece of metal pipe into the centre, leave it for about 15 minutes, then take it out (wearing gloves) and see if it's hot.

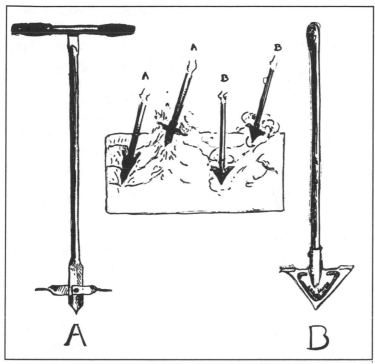

Two different kinds of commercially available aerating tools for mixing compost and getting air into the pile.

Stirring, Poking, Fluffing and Generally Agitating

These methods of aerating your pile are the lazy person's way of getting air into the pile and they work just fine. You can use a stick, an old broom handle, a shovel, a piece of pipe or a garden fork. Plunge the implement into the pile in many different places, as far as you can. (This also helps to break tough materials, providing easier access for decomposer organisms.) Try stirring the pile with the stick. If this is difficult, just move materials as much as you can. It's okay if you can't stir it like a soup; it's good enough just to make air holes, even temporary ones.

Some companies sell aerating tools. The best ones have end-flaps that fold out as you pull the tool out of the heap, thereby loosening materials. Watch that you don't hurt your back using these tools: position your feet properly before pulling the aerator out of the pile. Some tools have sharp ends, and they are good for breaking through tough materials.

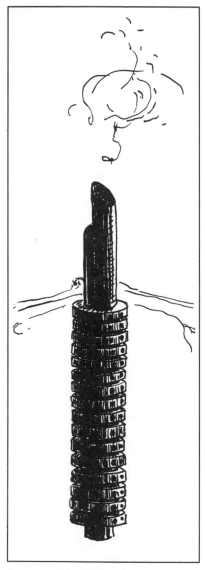

A commercial ventilation stack.

RULE OF THUMB

If your pile is too wet (moisture content above 60 percent, water draining out the bottom, or water dripping when you squeeze the compost), the aerobic bacteria may die off and smelly anaerobes take over. If the pile is too dry (moisture content below 40 percent, compost crumbles when you squeeze it), composting will be slow and the pile won't heat up. The ideal is to have compost as moist as a wrung-out sponge.

Air or Ventilating Stacks

Ventilating stacks are put in the pile while you're constructing it. They are usually perforated to allow for good air movement. You can use just one stack (or even three or four), and then you pile materials around the stack. If you're adding materials to the pile gradually, rather than building it all at once, the bottom layer should be thick enough to hold the stack in place. The advantage of stacks is that they ensure a good oxygen supply without the necessity of turning. Stacks can be made out of perforated pipe, a cylinder of wire mesh or even a bunch of twigs loosely tied together.

Commercial air stacks are available (see Sources for manufacturers and suppliers).

MOISTURE: THE SPONGE RULE

The microcommunity of bacteria and organisms in your compost pile needs water to live. Depending on the materials you put into your pile (wet materials like manure and kitchen scraps, or dry things like straw or sawdust), you may have to add water or take steps to dry out your pile. The best moisture content for compost is between 40 and 60 percent. Since you have no easy way of measuring this, the rule of thumb is that you should try to maintain the consistency of a wrung-out sponge in your heap. That is, under the top layer, which will probably be drier, the material should be damp and glistening, but if you squeeze it, no water should drain out. If it just crumbles and doesn't hold together at all when you squeeze it, the pile is probably too dry.

If your pile is not covered, too much rainwater and additions of wet materials may cause excessive moisture problems — specifically, anaerobic odour and loss of nutrients by leaching out the bottom. The best way to dry out a pile is by turning it, fluffing it, poking holes to get air in or adding dry material, like straw. During rainy periods, a cover will keep the pile dry; during sunnier times, keeping the pile exposed to the air will help dry out materials.

On the other hand, getting enough moisture to the centre of the pile is often a problem. Just soaking the pile with a hose doesn't ensure that the inside materials will get wet;

even when water starts running off the pile, it may have just penetrated a few inches, caking the top materials and preventing aeration. It's best to poke holes with a stick or broom handle first and then pour water into the holes.

FOOD FOR THOUGHT

Growing zucchini, pumpkin, cucumber or other melon crops on the top of your compost can be very rewarding. Cucurbits love heat, are heavy feeders, and having them there is a good reminder to water your compost regularly. As well, your compost will blossom and bear fruit throughout the summer — visual proof of your compost's fertile lushness.

Just plant seeds an inch or so deep on the outer edges of your heap and water regularly.

Water Tips

- Thoroughly soak dry materials as you layer them on the heap.
- Fresh green materials, especially when chopped into small pieces, probably won't need to be watered.
- Use unsalted vegetable cooking water (full of nutrients) to moisten your pile (but not dishwater, which may be greasy).
- If you're using the build-it-all-at-once compost method, then if you moisten the heap while you're piling it up, you probably won't have to add water later.
- When you turn your pile, do a moisture-squeeze test; if the pile seems dry, add water after you've turned materials (it won't be as heavy).
- Weeds growing in your pile steal moisture. Pull them out immediately and either dry them in the sun before putting them back on your pile or place them back on the pile with the roots up.
- If you live in a particularly wet area with lots of rainfall, try to round your pile so it sheds excess moisture.

- If you live in a dry area, or if it's a particularly dry summer, make a concave shape in the top of your pile so it traps and holds rain-water, and gradually lets it seep into the pile.

THE PILE'S pH: THE ACID TEST

The **pH scale** is a measure of **alkalinity** or **acidity**. If a material has a pH of 0, it is purely acidic; if the pH is 14, it is a purely alkaline or basic. A pH of 7, which is mid-way on the scale, indicates that it is neutral.

The bacteria living in a compost heap prefer a pH of from 6 to just over 7, or neutral, and it is best to keep your heap in this range. If you're adding a wide assortment of materials to your heap, you probably don't have to worry about pH at all; the mixture will likely have an ideal pH of close to 7.

		THE pH SCALE
	14.0	
	13.0	Caustic Soda
Alkaline	12.4	Lime (calcium hydroxide)
	11.0	Ammonia (NH_3)
	8.3	Sea Water
	7.4	Human Blood
	7.0	Neutral — Distilled Water
	6.6	Milk
Acidic	4.2	Carrots
	2.2	Vinegar
	1.0	Battery Acid
	0.0	

However, you can try to keep the pH neutral by balancing what goes into the heap, keeping in mind the relative acidity of materials. For example, if you're adding lots of acidic materials such as oak leaves or manure, try to balance these with some kind of alkaline material such as crushed limestone, bonemeal, crushed egg shell or wood ash. (For a list of the acidity and alkalinity of materials, see Chapter 6.)

You can also determine the pH level of your pile with a home soil-test kit or a pH-test kit. These come with a test ribbon and a colour chart, which will tell you the pH of the sample. (Home soil-test kits are available from garden centres.) You can then adjust the pH by adding acidic or alkaline material. Or, if you want more detailed results, you can send compost samples to a private, government or university lab for testing.

If you are measuring the pH yourself, you may get a reading that shows high acidity (i.e. a low pH of 4 or 5) if you test the compost too soon. The early stages of decomposition tend to produce slightly acidic conditions. This is a normal part of the pH cycle. As decomposition continues, the pile will neutralize on its own if it's getting enough oxygen. Therefore, it's not a good idea to test in the pile's first few weeks. Instead, it makes most sense to test finished compost and the pH of your garden soil. Compare the pH findings to the needs of the particular plants you intend to use in the garden, and *then* make adjustments to the soil with either lime (alkaline) or peat moss (acidic).

Chances are that, if anything, your heap will be more acidic than alkaline. An overly acidic heap can be balanced by adding crushed (granular) dolomitic limestone (available at garden centres) or some other alkaline material such as egg shells.

However, for the casual composter putting a good mix of food and/or garden scraps into the compost, it's quite possible to ignore pH altogether, or to worry about acidity and alkalinity *only* if you are experiencing specific problems (see troubleshooting suggestions in Chapter 7).

TO LIME OR NOT TO LIME

This is one of those controversial compost topics on which you'll get three different opinions from three different people. (Of course, controversy is a well-known gardening disease!) It may be best to do your own experiments with lime.

Some people put lime in their compost piles because it adds calcium, which is important to plants; keeps the acidity down; and controls odour. However, overliming your pile can be bad for the heap. It may lead to a loss of nitrogen, which will adversely affect the work of bacteria and the amount of this important nutrient that you'll have in your finished compost. If you've added lime and your heap starts to give off an ammonia odour, it probably means that you've added too much lime and you're losing nitrogen. Turn the pile and don't add any more lime.

However, if you suspect that your pile is acidic because you've been adding a lot of oak leaves or pine needles, for example, it's probably a good idea to add lime. A word of caution: don't use quicklime (calcium oxide), which is freshly burned lime. It's caustic.

CARBON:NITROGEN RATIO

The **carbon:nitrogen ratio** (**C:N ratio**) is a term that keeps popping up in any discussion of composting. Basically, all living things (or once-alive things) contain carbon and nitrogen. The ratio of carbon to nitrogen in a material is one of the most important factors that determine how quickly or slowly it will decompose. For example, a highly carbonaceous material such as dead wood breaks down slowly, because the ratio of carbon to nitrogen is very high. A material high in nitrogen, such as food waste or grass, breaks down faster.

However, it's not a good idea to make a compost pile only out of high-nitrogen materials. Although it would decompose quickly, it would be smelly and the heap would actually lose its nitrogen while decomposing. (When there is too much nitrogen in the pile, the nitrogen volatizes and escapes

---

RULE OF THUMB

As beneficial (and nitrogen rich) as food scraps and grass clippings are, for maximum benefit they should be layered or mixed equally in your compost with garden soil and a high-carbon material like dead leaves. And, as most gardeners already know, it's *far* better to leave grass clippings on your lawn, where they will break down and return nutrients directly to the growing grass.

into the air as ammonia.) This finished compost is not really useful as a nutrient source for growing plants. If, however, you live in the city, don't have garden wastes and the only compost material you have is food scraps (generally high in nitrogen), then by adding a 1" layer of soil on top of food-scrap additions you will be "trapping" the ammonia, keeping the nitrogen in the pile.

The ideal C:N ratio for your compost heap is from approximately 20:1 (20 parts of carbon to 1 part of nitrogen) to 30:1. That is, the micro-organisms in your heap use carbon and nitrogen in a ratio of approximately 20:1 to 30:1 during their growth. So, if you create a heap with this C:N ratio, the micro-organisms will be working at peak efficiency. You can achieve this balance in your heap by adding a mix of materials to your heap which includes those that are high in carbon and those that are high in nitrogen (see Chapter 6 for more details on the carbon:nitrogen ratio and how to balance your heap).

Just as the heap goes through a pH cycle and a temperature cycle, it also goes through a nitrogen cycle. In the early stages of decomposition, the bacteria are consuming nitrogen, so the amount of nitrogen in the pile will be temporarily low. However, as the bacteria keep working, they also excrete nitrogen. And as they die off, they contribute their nitrogen to the compost, raising the level again and making finished compost a good source of nitrogen for the garden.

Guide to Nutrients

In order to grow, plants get the chemicals (called **plant nutrients**) they need from the soil. Compost adds nutrients to the soil, and this is one of the reasons why compost is so good for your garden. The major, but certainly not the only, nutrients necessary for plant growth are nitrogen (N), phosphorus (P) and potassium (K). Many other nutrients and **trace elements** are minor or secondary, but are necessary in smaller amounts. When the soil is cultivated, the plants "take up" or deplete the soil of nutrients, and compost is an excellent way to recharge the garden.

Nitrogen:
Nitrogen is essential to the growth of all plants and may be the single most important plant nutrient. It is used primarily by the stems and leaves; without nitrogen, plant growth is stunted. Nitrogen can escape quickly, either as a gas or by being washed away, especially when it is added to soil in the form of an artificial fertilizer. The nitrogen in compost is stable and is therefore released slowly to plants as they need it.

Phosphorus:
This stimulates root growth and is necessary for fruit and flower growth in plants, and also for photosynthesis.

Potassium:
This is necessary for the development of chlorophyll, which is what makes photosynthesis possible. Potassium also strengthens plant tissue. In the form of potash, potassium can easily wash out of compost (because of rain, for example). This is why it's important to cover additions of wood ash to compost with some other material, such as soil.

Nutrients and Commercial Fertilizers

When you buy commercial fertilizers, the NPK numbers on the package (e.g. 21-7-7) show the ratios of these three major nutrients in the fertilizer. The NPK content of finished compost varies from one pile to another and it may, in some instances, be lower than that found in commercial fertilizers. (Only a soil test from a lab will give you the actual NPK content of your compost. Curious gardeners may want to send samples for testing.) However, the value of compost is that the nutrients are stored in your garden soil and released slowly. This makes the nutrients available to plants longer than the "quick fix" that is provided by commercial fertilizers. Even "slow release" fertilizers are no substitute for compost: fertilizers provide the major nutrients, but they do not add any organic matter or microbial life to the soil as compost does.

■ 6 ■

Recipe for a Healthy Heap

When you add kitchen garbage to your compost pile, you're recovering a lot of nutrition that you used to waste. For instance, the average Canadian family throws away every year as much iron as is contained in 500 eggs, as much protein as they'd get from 60 steaks, and a volume of vitamins equal to the contents of 95 glasses of orange juice — just in discarded potato peelings.

— Pollution Probe
The Canadian Green Consumer Guide

What goes into your compost pile is the single most important factor affecting the quality of the composting process and the end result. The key is to have a balance of materials high in carbon and materials high in nitrogen. The greater the variety of materials you add to your heap, the better your chances of achieving a good carbon:nitrogen ratio, the greater the variety of micro-organisms in your heap and the more nicely balanced the finished humus.

Anything organic — that is, anything that is or was once living — will eventually decompose. Even a wooden house will decompose; it will just take a very long time. (We know what happened to the dinosaurs: a few of their bones fossilized, but everything else composted over time.)

In the controlled environment of your heap or pile, you are trying to create the best conditions for the decomposition process, conditions that ensure speedy and complete breakdown and destruction of any pathogens (organisms that cause diseases) that might be present. Therefore, there are some organic materials that you should not put on the heap, others that you should use only in moderation and others that are best added only when combined with other materials. If this sounds as if you need a science degree to compost, don't worry — there are only a few rules to follow, and many of them are common sense.

You can compost most organic materials that you put in the garbage: most food scraps, garden wastes and lawn clippings. These materials probably account for about a third of your garbage.

VARIETY MEANS QUALITY

The key to good composting (and a good finished product) is diversity of materials: the more variety you put into your heap, the better the compost that comes out. Everything organic has carbon and nitrogen in its tissues. The carbon: nitrogen ratio (C:N) of materials is a major factor affecting the time they take to break down. The first number is the parts of carbon in relation to one part of nitrogen (for example, 25 carbon: 1 nitrogen). Sometimes, people leave off the one part nitrogen and state it as just the carbon amount (e.g. 25).

The ideal C:N for composting is from around 20:1 to 30:1. If your pile is made up primarily of carbonaceous materials (C:N of 40:1) like dead leaves, then the pile will stay cool and it will take longer for the materials to break down. If the pile is high in nitrogen (a lower C:N of 10:1 for example) with too many grass clippings, the pile may smell like ammonia and perhaps turn slimy.

Because most people don't have a precise way to measure the C:N of their piles, it's fine to go by trial and error and to follow general rules of thumb rather than to worry about achieving an exact ratio. For example, when you add high carbon materials such as dead leaves or wood chips, you should balance them with some high nitrogen material such as food waste. (Doing your rough figuring by weight will give you better results, but since people rarely weigh their wastes, you can go by volume.) For example, if you add dead leaves (with a C:N of approximately 40:1) and then add a similar weight of grass clippings (20:1), you will probably have an ideal ratio of 30:1

You don't have to memorize the carbon:nitrogen ratio of all materials in order to make good, fast compost. And anyway, there will be a wide variety of C:Ns within materials of the same type. Instead, you can think of materials as either "browns" (high in carbon) or "greens" (high in nitrogen) and try to balance them. Browns are usually fibrous and greens less fibrous. (The following lists rough C:Ns — there is always variety.)

Browns: dead leaves (40:1 to 80:1), straw (80:1), cornstalks (60:1), sawdust (150:1 to 500:1), wood chips (500:1 to 700:1), paper (170:1).

Greens: food scraps (15:1), fresh grass clippings (19:1), rotted manure (20:1), fruit waste (35:1).

Some materials are both browns and greens. For example, fresh grass clippings and fresh leaves are greens, but dried grass clippings and dead leaves are browns.

The mixing of browns and greens is important not just for the C:N ratio, but also because different sizes, textures and chemical compositions of materials make for better compost structure, drainage and nutrient content.

Another quick (but not foolproof) way to differentiate between carbon and nitrogen materials is to remember that materials of animal origin (such as feathers, manure, blood-meal) are usually high in nitrogen, while dried materials of vegetable origin are usually high in carbon. (However, most fresh food wastes are high in nitrogen.)

If your goal is to make compost quickly (e.g. the 14-day method, see Chapter 3), you will have to be more cautious and precise about the C:N ratio. But for most composting, it's okay to guess at the balance by varying the browns and greens by rough weight and making observations about the results. If there's a problem in the balance, you'll smell it (too much nitrogen) or you'll see that the decomposition process is moving slowly (too much carbon).

Think of composting as a kind of cooking: some people follow recipes to the letter, others cook by trial and error. You can find the method that suits you best.

Storing Compostables

A messy question: where to store kitchen scraps before taking them out to the compost bin? A familiar sight in many composting homes is a container beside the kitchen sink for scraps. When it fills up, empty the container into the bin. A small bucket with a lid, such as a recycled ice cream or lard pail, works well and helps to control fruit flies in the summer. (Fruit flies love to flit around kitchen scraps.) Ceramic containers with lids (such as those sold at kitchen supply stores) seem to control odours better than plastic containers.

If you find it more convenient, you may want to place the container beside your regular garbage bin, so you get into the garbage-separating habit.

"Designer" kitchen collectors are also available commercially. For example, some systems use color-coded small bins that can be mounted onto kitchen cupboards—the bin for compostables is usually green, with other bins for metals and glass, etc. A five-quart kitchen compost holder (9″ high) with lid is also available by mail order from Gardener's Eden (see Sources).

If you are one of the unfortunate many who share their living quarters with multi-legged creatures such as roaches, it's best not to keep your storing container for compostables in a dark, humid place, like under the sink. And you'll need a lid. You may want to keep your container in the refrigerator or freezer — completely pest-proof.

COMPOSTABLE MATERIALS: A PARTIAL LIST

A complete list of compostables would fill a book, so the following section is limited to some common materials. Where an item is a particularly good source of one or more nutrients, this information has been included for your interest.

Algae: good nutrient source

Alfalfa: good nitrogen source

Asparagus

Bananas and skins: phosphoric acid and potash

Beet tops: calcium and magnesium, nitrogen

Berries

Bloodmeal: nitrogen

Bonemeal: phosphorus, nitrogen

Citrus rinds: potash

Coffee grounds and filter: acidic, preserve moisture well, nitrogen, deodorize compost

Corn cobs: shred, take a long time to decompose but good for structure

Egg shells: crush, alkalizer (neutralizes acidic materials), calcium

Feathers: nitrogen

Flowers

Garden refuse: when fresh, good mix of carbon and nitrogen; when dried, mostly carbon

Granite dust: potash

Grapes

Grass: nitrogen (fresh grass clippings), carbon (dried grass clippings)

Hair: (avoid chemically dyed hair), nitrogen

Hay: will soak up moisture; you may need to add water

Hoof and horn meal: nitrogen

Leaves: carbon

Limestone: alkalizer

Manure: nitrogen
Oats: nitrogen
Peanut shells: potassium
Peat moss: acidic, organic material for soil building and
  water retention, little nutrient value
Phosphate rock: phosphorous and mineral elements
Potash rock: potassium
Potato: potash
Sawdust: carbon
Seaweed: potassium
Soil: minerals, micro-organisms
Straw: carbon, organic material
Tea grounds and leaves: nitrogen
Weeds: nitrogen, phosphorous, organic material
Wood ash: potash, alkalizer

DEALING WITH COMMON INGREDIENTS
As you experiment with different materials, you will discover
special tricks and rules, but the following are some guidelines
for dealing with common composting ingredients.

Garden Scraps:
These should be chopped into small pieces. Watch out for
weeds that have gone to seed and diseased plants: if the temperature in your heap doesn't reach the 70° C (160° F) range,
the seeds and disease-causing pathogens will not be killed.
Branches and hedge trimmings will take forever to decompose unless they are chopped or shredded. Once chipped,
they break down faster. If you're using a lot of leaves in your
pile, keep them well aerated because leaves tend to mat and
become anaerobic. For best results, mix with other materials.

Grass:
It's best to leave grass clippings on your lawn, where they
will add their nutrients directly to the lawn. (Short cuttings
will not smother the lawn or form thatch.) However, grass

clippings are a good source of nitrogen in a compost heap, but they can turn smelly and slimy if they mat. To avoid this, let them dry out for a few days first and then add to compost. Or, add them to the compost when they are green, but fluff them up with an absorbant material like leaves or straw, then add a one-inch layer of soil. Grass clippings should always go on the heap in thin layers, alternated with other materials such as kitchen scraps or dead leaves. If you're pulling up sod and adding it to the compost, put the grass side down and the roots up to dry it out.

Hay or Straw:
These are best used after being weathered first. You will have to add water to these materials.

Kitchen Scraps:
All kitchen scraps decompose faster if chopped into small pieces of about one-inch square. This is particularly important for stringy or tough scraps such as celery, artichoke leaves, grapefruit rinds, etc. Egg shells should be crushed. Avoid greasy or oil-laden scraps: they take a long time to break down, will possibly smell bad and may attract pests.

Leaves:
There are many different ways you can compost leaves: in your regular heap as a good carbon source, in their own

CARBON:NITROGEN RATIO OF LEAVES			
Alder	15:1	Larch	113:1
Ash	21:1	Linden	37:1
Aspen	63:1	Maple	52:1
Beech	51:1	Oak	47:1
Birch	50:1	Pine	66:1
Black Elder	22:1	Red Oak	53:1
Douglas Fir	77:1	Spruce	48:1
Elm	28:1		

Source: Friedrich Schaller, *Soil Animals*

heap, or as a mulch. (See "Leaves: Special Compost Treatments" later in this chapter for more information.)

Manure:

Manure from vegetarian animals (cows, sheep, horses, etc.) is an excellent source of nitrogen and moisture for your pile. The high bacterial population in manure gets the heap working quickly. Rotted or composted manure is best because the nitrogen is "fixed," whereas nitrogen can leach out of fresh manure. The nutrient content varies for different types of manures. For example, chicken and rabbit manures are richest in nitrogen, and horse and sheep manures are richer in nitrogen than cow or hog manures. Manure is best layered with carbonaceous materials such as dead leaves or straw, and manure's high nitrogen content will ensure rapid decomposition of these carbon materials.

ESTIMATED NITROGEN CONTENT OF VARIOUS MANURES

The nutrient content of manure varies among animal species and depends on the animal's diet. The following chart lists the relative nitrogen content of different kinds of manure. (It's worth noting that one dairy cow excretes about 20 tons of manure a year.)

Animal Manure	Percent Nitrogen	Animal Manure	Percent Nitrogen
Rabbit	2.4	Horse	0.7
Hen	1.1	Duck	0.6
Sheep	0.7	Cow	0.6
Steer	0.7	Pig	0.5

Source: Jerry Minnich et al., *The Rodale Guide to Composting*

Sawdust:

Don't add too much at once. If layers are more than one inch or so, the sawdust may mat and prevent aeration. It's also best to layer with a nitrogen-rich material. Sawdust breaks down relatively slowly, and gobbles up nitrogen in the process.

Weeds:
If the weeds haven't gone to seed, then add them to any pile. But if they have gone to seed, you have to ensure adequate heat in the pile in order to kill off the weed seeds. Add manure and make sure that the weeds are in the hot centre of the pile. If they're on the surface of the pile, they may start to grow again. Some gardeners burn weeds that have gone to seed and diseased plants, then add the ash to the soil. Since open burning is illegal in many urban areas, check with your fire department first.

Wood Ash:
If you have a fireplace, wood ash is a great source of potash for compost, but don't add too much at once. A thin sprinkling layered with other materials is best. Also, potash leaches out with rain so this layer should be covered. If you are adding burned material to your compost pile, avoid coated papers or coloured inks, which may have heavy metals in their ashes.

MATERIALS TO AVOID
Although the general rule is that any material that was once living can be composted, there are a number of organic materials that can cause problems in your compost. What follows are some general guidelines. Again, you may want to experiment. For example, some people have no problems if they add dairy products in moderation. However, the animal fats may attract pests and they may smell. If you live in a dense urban area, it's not worth taking the risk.

A heap made with a variety of materials is best in terms of structure and nutrient content. Therefore, if you can, avoid making the heap out of all one material. (However, see "Leaves: Special Compost Treatments" later in this chapter for making a leaf pile.)

On the left, materials that can be put on a compost pile. On the right, materials that should be avoided.

Bones:
Not only do they take a long time to break down, but they will attract pests.

Cat Litter:
Although it seems like a waste to throw this out, cat litter should not be composted for two reasons: the pathogens that are a problem in cat feces can survive in cat litter, and chemicals to perfume the litter or to keep the dust down are sometimes added to cat litter.

Charcoal and Briquets:
If it's pure wood charcoal, there's no problem, but some manufacturers add chemicals to make the charcoal burn faster. Read the fine print, phone the manufacturer or avoid this material altogether.

Coal Ashes:
May contain toxic amounts — toxic to the plants on which you'll use your finished compost — of sulphur and iron.

Contaminated Materials:
Avoid grass or plant material that has been sprayed with herbicides, pesticides, insecticides or fungicides. The degradability and toxicity of different chemicals vary greatly, so it's best not to use any **synthetic chemicals** on your garden that may contaminate compostable materials and the finished compost. If you're collecting compost materials along roadsides, be aware that herbicides are sometimes applied by your local highway work crews.

Dairy:
These products may smell, take a long time to decompose, and attract pests.

Fatty, Oily Foods:
These materials may smell and will take a long time to break down. As well, they may attract pests. You can try experimenting with these materials in moderation, adding a layer of soil to completely cover them.

Fish:
Like meat, this will attract pests and smell.

Meat:
Meat will attract pests and may smell when decomposing. Some manufacturers of commercial bins called "digesters" say that it's okay to add meat, but unless the bin is absolutely rodent proof (with screening underneath and around sides and a tight-fitting lid), adding meat will cause problems.

Newspapers:
If you live in an area with recycling facilities for newspapers, it makes more sense to recycle newspapers than to compost them. Also, there may be heavy metals in the coloured inks and coated paper stock. However, if you still want to compost newspaper, it will break down faster if shredded and mixed with food waste.

Pet Wastes, Human Excrement:
These manures may contain pathogenic bacteria, viruses and parasites that require high temperatures to be destroyed. Because you can't be absolutely certain that these high temperatures are reached throughout the pile, it's best not to use them, especially if you are applying the finished compost to edible plants and garden vegetables. However, some people have a separate compost pile for ornamental plants, in which they put pet waste (though not when the animal is sick). Even so, such compost is best buried at least six to eight inches into the ground.

Rhubarb Leaves:
There is some controversy about rhubarb leaves, because they may be toxic to other plants. Some gardeners use them for compost with no visible ill effects in the garden, but other gardeners won't use them. As a raw material, fresh rhubarb leaves *are* poisonous to humans.

Weed Seeds and Diseased Plants:
Try to put weeds on your compost pile *before* they go to seed. Unless you are making a hot heap that reaches at least 70° C (160° F), the weed seeds will survive the composting process. Disease-causing organisms may survive the composting process.

HARD TO COMPOST, BUT COMPOSTABLE
The main problem with some "difficult-to-compost" materials is that they take a long time to break down. This doesn't mean that you shouldn't use them, only that special care should be taken. You should know in advance that you may be seeing these materials over and over again when you turn your pile over and over.

Corn cobs, for example, may take a few years to break down. However, as with any material, they will break down faster if you chop them first and mix them with high-nitrogen materials. When harvesting your compost, screen out the cobs and crumble them in your hands and put them back in the pile or use them on your garden with the rest of the compost.

Nut shells and pits will also take a while, but it's fine to add them. Other materials that decompose slowly include pieces of dead wood (though "green" wood that is freshly cut or chipped breaks down well if mixed with a high-nitrogen material), oyster and clam shells, cotton rags and wine corks.

Many people advise against adding highly acidic material in large amounts to compost heaps. However, if you have a lot of pine needles, oak leaves, etc. there's no reason not to compost them. Layer with other materials such as manure, food scraps or grass clippings. And, if they still don't break down, you can always add lime or lots of crushed egg shells to neutralize the acidic conditions. On the other hand, you may want to deliberately make acidic compost for acid-loving plants. (See "Compost Concoctions for Special Plants" in Chapter 8.)

Another hard-to-compost-but-compostable material falls into this category not because it breaks down slowly, but because you have to take extra care over pathogens. Human urine is usually sterile when it leaves the body, unless you have a bladder or kidney infection. It is a source of nitrogen, so it should only be added to heaps that have a lot of carbon materials and only if no infections are present.

FORAGING: FINDING COMPOSTABLES

Although some people may find it difficult to imagine not having enough garbage, others may want to forage around in the community to supplement the materials going into their heaps. This is a great way to "save" garbage from landfill, to recycle wasted organic material back into the soil and to add variety to your heap. Someone's trash may be your compost treasure! They may be thrilled to have you take it away; it may actually lower their disposal costs.

Food Wastes:
Good sources are local supermarkets and green grocers, restaurants and hotels, daycare centres, office lunchrooms and cafeterias.

Hair:
Barbershops and beauty parlours, but you don't want hair that has been chemically treated or coloured.

Manure:
Riding stables, race tracks, police stables and local farmers.

Plant Wastes:
Local florists (beware of chemical contamination), neighbours, city works departments, landscape companies and
parks departments. If you're collecting plant wastes from the
wild, be careful not to take living plants. Also, if collecting
from a roadside or highway area, make sure that the plants
haven't been sprayed.

Sawdust and Wood Shavings:
Lumber mills may give this to you, but make sure that the
shavings are from untreated wood. Tree pruning services
may deliver at no cost.

Please keep in mind that if you get your compostables
from other sources, you lose control over what goes into your
pile (and you may be getting into some pretty grey legal and
health regulation areas). For example, food wastes from
restaurants may be contaminated with cockroaches and rat
droppings. Manure from race tracks and stables may be high
in antibiotics. Florists may use chemicals on their plants. All
things considered, you may decide that the benefits aren't
worth the risks.

LEAVES: SPECIAL COMPOST TREATMENTS
People who make compost usually balk at the sight of all
those bags of leaves at the curbside in the fall. They can't
understand why people are throwing out all those good-as-
gold leaves. Instead of sending them on a one-way trip to
landfill, you can recycle their nutrients back into the soil.

> When I drive along city streets in the fall and see great
> trucks hauling away all the leaves I could weep, and so
> could your flowers and shrubs.
> — Midge Ellis Keeble, *Tottering in My Garden*

In fact, many communities are banning leaves from landfill sites. Some cities have central composting facilities for leaves; residents bundle them in bags for curbside collection. However, it makes much more sense to make your leaves work for *you*, with backyard composting.

There are many different ways you can compost your leaves:

- Add them to your heap as a carbon source to balance nitrogen-rich additions of manure or food wastes.
- Have a separate heap for leaves.
- Make leaf mould in a garbage can or bag.
- Use leaves as garden mulch to insulate soil and prevent weeds.
- Dig leaves into the garden in fall.

Leaves in Your Regular Compost Pile:

Leaves are a good source of carbon and organic material. However, you shouldn't add them all at once. Layers over eight inches may compact and prevent air circulation, and provide too much carbon all at once. Instead, use the greens and browns rule. That is, add a layer of food scraps, bloodmeal, green grass clippings, or — perhaps most practical of all — spent annual flowering plants and vegetable plants (you're likely pulling these up at about the same time as you are gathering leaves), perennial cuttings or manure, to balance the addition of leaves. You can collect your leaves all at once and then keep a bushelful by the heap so you can add them gradually: just toss some on the heap after you add food scraps. If you have a lawn mower and the energy, you can shred leaves first, though it's not strictly necessary.

Leaf Heaps:

Leaves add valuable materials to the soil: they add fibrous organic matter, enabling the soil to hold moisture and air better, and they add essential minerals.

If you have a lot of leaves to compost, it may be a good idea to have a separate leaf pile. It should be relatively large (four feet in diameter, three feet in height), though leaves will reduce in volume quite quickly, and it should be out of the wind.

You can make a simple leaf heap container using snow fencing or wire mesh. (The compost should be ready in a year.) Put the wire or fencing in a circle. Build a pile of leaves inside, adding a thin layer of soil every six inches or so and water each layer. Shredding your leaves (using your lawn mower at its highest setting) will speed up decomposition.

If you're using predominantly acidic leaves such as oak, you may want to add powdered lime, one or two cups (for the whole pile), when you're adding leaves. To balance the high carbon content of leaves, you could also put one part manure to five parts of leaves in the pile. Instead of manure, you can also use other high nitrogen materials such as one or two cups of bloodmeal per wheelbarrowful of leaves. Add water to the leaf layers when building the heap. Cover with wire over the winter. In the spring, remove wire and add a few shovelfuls of manure and soil or 3 or 4 lbs (2 kg) of blood meal or bonemeal. If the mass seems compacted or smelly, turn the leaves over to dry them out. If the pile gets too dry over the summer, add water. The compost should be ready to be dug into the garden by the fall or the next spring.

Some leaf piles, such as those made with oak and chestnut, may take up to two years to decompose. So, you may want to have two piles: one for the first fall's leaves, the other for next year's. (One pile will be full of finished compost rather than having to dig it out from underneath the second year's decomposing leaves.)

Leaf Mould:

Leaf mould (decomposed leaves) is excellent for digging into the garden. It improves the water-holding capability of soil and is a good conditioner. As well, leaf mould can be made very easily. If you start in the fall, you should have some ready by the next fall. All you need is leaves and either a sturdy garbage bag or can. Though not absolutely necessary, it's best to shred the leaves first. Place them in a garbage can or bag, tamp them down, moisten, close the bag and leave it in an out-of-the-way corner (sunny if possible). By spring, the leaves will have started to turn into leaf mould, and this can now be dug into the garden or added to your regular compost heap for further decomposition. Or, you can wait until the fall when the leaves have turned into leaf mould.

Leaves as Mulch:
Mulch is any layer of material on top of the soil. Though it's best to mulch with an organic material that will break down and add its nutrients to the soil, some people use old carpets or plastic as mulch. Mulch is used to conserve soil moisture, keep soil temperature steady, reduce growth of weeds and prevent erosion. Leaves can be put on the soil as mulch in the fall and then dug into the garden in spring (they will be partially decomposed). Or, they can be used as mulch in the spring, to protect seedlings.

Leaves can also be left on the lawn, but only if well shredded. A mulching lawn mower is best for shredding. Acidic leaves can be shredded and placed as a winter mulch around acid-loving plants. Some gardeners have great success putting leaves as a mulch over root crops in the fall (carrots, parsnips, etc.) and then they are able to pull up their vegetables well into the winter.

Dig in Your Leaves:
When you add dead leaves directly to the soil without composting them first, the microbes that decompose the leaves take away nitrogen temporarily from growing plants. However, if you dig leaves into soil in the fall, the decomposition should occur over the winter and the nitrogen

should be available for plants by spring. Or, you can supplement the nitrogen loss with bonemeal or bloodmeal in the
spring.

This method will be a lot of work if you have a huge
volume of leaves.

As you can see, these compost ingredients — leaves, food
wastes, garden scraps — are far too valuable to throw out as
garbage. You'll find that you start to see "raw materials"
everywhere, mouthwatering wastes (if you're really far
gone!) that other people see as disposal problems. You may
even become possessive about your organic materials.

Toronto fiction writer Sarah Sheard has written a wonderful story, "What Goes Around" (*The Journal of Wild
Culture*, Fall 1989), that gets at the heart of compost enthu-
siasm. In the story, the character finds herself scrutinizing
people's plates, assessing food scraps, longing to carry them
off to her own compost pile. You may start to recognize the
feeling . . .

■ 7 ■

Troubleshooting: Problems and Solutions

Somewhere in the history of composting we got the idea that, if left alone, Mother Nature would be odor free. I don't know how this idea arose, but I assure you that it's not true ... As the song says, 'the buffalo roamed,' and they did so for very good reason.
— Roger T. Haug, *BioCycle* (October 1990)

There are few things that discourage someone from starting a compost heap more than having suffered through the stench of a neighbour's heap gone wrong. And few things are more embarrassing than proudly displaying your compost pile to a friend, only to have a mouse jump out! And, of course, it's very discouraging to build a pile only to wait, and wait, for finished compost that never seems to appear. But take heart, composting problems are easy to fix. The trick is to learn to read the symptoms and to experiment with remedies.

In general, composting problems tend to fall into three broad categories: odour problems, pest problems, and slow decomposition problems. All are related to the composting variables: the size and kinds of materials you put in your pile, moisture level, and ventilation. If you're having a problem, it probably means that one or more of these variables is out of balance and needs to be adjusted.

Think of compost problems as your compost pile's way of communicating with you. Compost sends you signals that something is wrong — by smelling bad, or drying up or decaying slowly. Answer back with the right remedy.

SYMPTOM: STINKY COMPOST

Although composting will never be completely odour free, one of the most prevalent misconceptions is that composting stinks. A good heap will not smell bad, even though what's going on in the pile is, simply, rotting. Finished compost has an extremely pleasant, some would say comforting, odour of sweet earth — much like the sweet scent of the forest floor in spring time, about the time of trillium blossoms and fiddlehead ferns.

If your compost pile starts to smell unpleasant, something has gone wrong. You'll be doing a favour to composting's good name if you take immediate steps to rectify the problem. As Carl Grimm, from the San Francisco League of Urban Gardeners, says, "The degree to which a system smells is the degree to which you neglect it" (*Recycling Today*, March 1991).

A stinky compost pile usually means that anaerobic bacteria have moved in. They'll still do your decomposing work for you but, in the process, make life miserable. Anaerobes give off a rotten-egg odour, and they take over when the pile isn't getting enough air, because it's too wet or too compacted.

Both causes of odour will be eliminated by turning, fluffing, poking or stirring your compost — by getting some air in. If your compost seems too wet, you can also add dry leaves or other dry organic material (e.g. shredded newspaper) to absorb excess moisture.

Some quick fixes for dealing with minor odour problems include keeping a one-inch layer of soil on top of the pile at all times, burying food waste under this layer, or putting a very thin layer of soil on top of every addition of food scraps. If you don't have extra soil, you can use some finished compost from the bottom of your pile. Or, you can add a sprinkling of lime (available from garden stores). However, lime may rob your heap of nitrogen, making the nitrogen content of your finished compost lower and therefore decreasing its effectiveness as a soil conditioner. Lime eliminates odour well, so you may decide that your ideal compost is an odourless heap rather than nitrogen-rich humus.

SYMPTOM: AMMONIA ODOUR

If you can identify an ammonia smell, it's actually not caused by anaerobes but because the pile has too many "greens," that is, too much nitrogen. This is not a big problem in itself, it just means that nitrogen is being lost in the form of ammonia gas, rather than being available for plants in the finished compost.

If you find the ammonia odour a problem, or if you don't want to lose nitrogen, add more carbon materials. If you don't have a ready supply of carbon materials, you can add some soil to absorb the ammonia gas or turn the pile to release the gas.

SYMPTOM: SLOW COMPOSTING

If you've been diligently building your pile out of chopped materials but nothing seems to be happening, a variety of reasons could account for the delay. It could be because the pile lacks nitrogen, particularly if you've been adding a lot of dried leaves. To get things "cooking," add some nitrogen-rich materials: food scraps, manure, green grass clippings or bloodmeal.

Slow decomposition may also be caused by turning the pile too often (more than once a week). Let it sit for a while and give the micro-organisms a chance to regroup and get working.

If you have a commercial bin (often smaller than 3'x3'x3'), decomposition could be slow until you build up a lot of materials.

SYMPTOM: PESTS

The faster and hotter your pile is, the less likely it is that you'll attract pests. However, raccoons, rats, mice, flies, etc. are all attracted to compost piles for food and refuge. Obviously, you have to make it difficult for pests to get at the food. As a preventative measure, always cover additions of food scraps with a thin layer of soil, or dig the food into the pile. If you know that there are raccoons or rats in your area, don't add meat, fish or bones to your pile. They'll immediately be attracted to your heap.

Rats

The only sure way to keep rats out is to **pest-proof** your bin, which makes it much more difficult for the creatures to invade. Pest-proofing takes work, but it's worth it in the long run. Wire mesh and half-inch or quarter-inch hard-

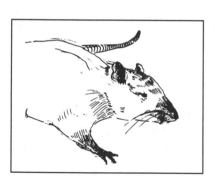

ware cloth work well. (Chicken wire is not rodent proof.) You'll have to put the mesh underneath the pile, around the sides and also on top — your bin should turn into a compost cage. (This is best done when you originally set up your bin, otherwise you'll have to dig the whole thing up.) In an urban area particularly, it's important to do everything possible to keep rats out. If you've got them, you may have to resort to traps and then pest-proof your bin with hardware cloth to make sure that these rodents don't come back. If you're thinking of setting out poison, call your local health department first. If your rat problem persists, you may want to use your outdoor compost pile for garden wastes only, and then compost food wastes indoors with a worm bin. Some cities have banned outdoor composting of food waste, so check with city hall.

As Michael Levenston, the executive director of City Farmer, an urban gardening education group in Vancouver, has pointed out, "If in five years everyone has turned their home garden into a landfill site, then we'll have lots of places for rats to hang out — unless people use rodent-resistant bins." City Farmer has paid particular attention to pest-proofing compost bins and they are an excellent source of information. They recommend that all urban composters make their bins rodent-resistant right from the start, when first setting up a bin. They sell a rodent-resistant compost bin kit, which includes a length of wire mesh, a plastic lid, and an information-packed booklet called *Urban Home Composting*, which includes three different plans for making your bin rodent resistant. (For more information, see Sources at the back of this book.)

Mice
Especially in winter, mice might find your pile a cozy place for nesting. In general, the less hospitable you make the pile — by keeping the pile as hot as possible or by poking holes into the pile and therefore into the mouse nests every few days — the less likely it is pests will camp out in your compost. However, before you go to a lot of trouble to get rid of mice, you may want to ask yourself if they really *are* a problem. Perhaps it makes sense to put up with them in the compost if it means they're not as interested in your house!

Raccoons
Raccoons tend to get into bins from the top, so secure the lid with a bungee cord.

If nothing seems to discourage the pests, you may want to consider composting indoors with worms, or on the porch or balcony with a garbage can and air stack.

Flies and Bugs

Soil (fungus) gnats and fruit flies may be a nuisance, but they can generally be controlled by covering all food scraps with soil. Flies seem to love damp hay and straw, which provide a good breeding ground. Again, cover with soil. If tiny fruit flies are busily buzzing around your compost, don't be alarmed. They are a part of the chain of decomposer organisms. An abundance of them is a sign that the surface of your compost needs a layer of garden topsoil.

Although it's next to impossible to control the bugs that live in your heap (after all, they are decomposer organisms helping the process along), there are two kinds that you may want to eliminate: cockroaches and earwigs. Luckily, infestations of both are relatively rare. In the north, cockroaches tend to live indoors, so the only ones you'll find in your heap probably hitchhiked in your food scrap container, which many people leave beside the sink. (If your bin is beside a shed or wall, roaches might be getting into the compost from these sources.) If these creatures are unwelcome in your heap, you can sprinkle diatomaceous earth (available at garden centres) around the heap. And to prevent future infestations, you can store food wastes in a container in the refrigerator rather than on or under a counter.

Because earwigs eat decaying material and dead insects, they actually help the compost process. However, gardeners may want to get rid of every earwig within 20 feet of their plants. You can use the same methods of control that you use for earwigs in the garden: traps. Place hollow tubes or pieces of crumpled newspaper around the heap; earwigs will climb in to hide. In the early morning, empty the bugs that have congregated inside into a dish of soapy water, where they will drown. Follow this procedure every morning until you get rid of the problem. (Some people use saucers of beer to attract earwigs. They climb in for a drink and never come out again.)

READING TROUBLE SIGNS

Symptom: Compost heap smells horrible.
Causes: Not enough air.
Too wet.
Solutions: Turn heap, poke air holes, or stir.
Add dry, carbon materials such as dead leaves.

Symptom: Materials aren't breaking down.
Causes: Pile too small and therefore not generating and keeping in enough heat.
Not enough nitrogen.
Not enough water.
Materials put into the pile are too large.
Solutions: Build heap at least 3'x3'x3'.
Add grass clippings, bloodmeal or manure.
Moisten heap to level of wrung-out sponge.
Chop materials into 1" pieces.

Symptom: Pests attracted to heap.
Causes: Wrong food added.
Food not buried properly.
Bin not rodent proof.
Solutions: Don't use meat, bones, fish or greasy scraps.
Add a thin non-food layer (e.g. soil, leaves) to each addition of food scraps or keep a non-food covering layer on the pile at all times and add food underneath it.
Bury food scraps in the centre of the heap.
Pest-proof your bin with hardware cloth.
Consider composting inside with a worm bin, or set up a garbage can with air stack on your porch or balcony, or use an off-the-ground drum rotating composter.

Symptom: Compost heap smells like ammonia.
Cause: Too much nitrogen.

Solution: Add carbon-rich materials such as straw, dead leaves.

Symptom: Pale green mould.
Cause: Lack of oxygen.
Solution: Turn pile, add lime.

Symptom: Lots of ants.
Cause: Pile too dry.
Solution: Add water and fresh cucumber peels.

COMMON COMPOSTING QUESTIONS

How long does it take to make compost?

It depends on the composting method you choose and what you put into your compost pile. However, most commercial or homemade bins that have been fed a mix of food waste, dead leaves and garden clippings will produce finished compost in approximately three to six months.

The fastest composting method is the 14-day turning pile (see Chapter 3). The slowest method is probably a compost pile that is filled only with dead leaves, which can take about a year to decompose.

Is it okay to add materials to a compost pile in winter? What if the heap freezes?

You can add materials to your pile throughout the year. The compost process will slow down in winter, and sometimes stop altogether, but the freeze/thaw cycle helps to break down materials and makes them decompose faster in the spring, when the pile really gets going again. Don't worry if the pile freezes.

If you want to extend the composting season into the winter, you can insulate your pile with dead leaves, straw or black plastic sheeting.

What is the best commercial bin?

Although all commercial bins work on similar principles,

they do have different features. Some commercial bins can handle meat, bones and dairy wastes; others won't. With some, you should turn the composting materials; with others, you don't have to. Some can go on a balcony; others can't. Which commercial bin is best for you depends on what you want to add to your compost pile, how long you want the process to take, how much time you have and how much room you have for the bin.

When you've answered these questions and reviewed the different bin features listed in Chapter 3, you should have the ideal commercial bin for your particular composting needs.

What is the best way to compost huge amounts of dead leaves and grass clippings?

If you have tons of leaves in the fall, you can make a separate leaf pile, enclosed with wire mesh. Or, you can store the leaves in bags and add them to your regular compost pile gradually over the year as a good carbon source for the compost.

Ideally, grass clippings should be left on the lawn, where they do the most good. (They return their nutrients to the growing grass.) However, you can add them to your compost pile because they're a good source of nitrogen for the compost. Or, you can make a separate pile enclosed with wire mesh, alternating layers of grass clippings with layers of dead leaves and soil.

Do I need to buy a commercial compost accelerator?

Compost accelerators are recommended by the manufacturers of some commercial bins (for example, the Green Cone). However, for most composters, they are not necessary for aerobic compost bins, particularly if you're not in a rush for your finished compost.

If you're starting a pile in the winter, you may want to use some compost accelerator to get things going.

What can I put in the compost pile?

Basically, anything that is, or once was, living. The

exceptions include meat, fish, bones, dairy, diseased plant materials, pet feces, and cat litter.

Why can't I put meat on the compost pile?

Meat, bones and fish will decompose. The problem is that in the process, they will also attract animals to your pile. And, with meat, disease-causing organisms may get into the compost pile and not be killed by the composting process.

Why can't I compost cat litter?

Again, disease-causing organisms are often found in pet feces and cat litter. These will only be killed by the composting process if you ensure very high temperatures in the pile — something that backyard composters rarely achieve. To be safe, put pet feces into the regular sewage system, which is designed to handle such wastes.

Can I put fireplace ash and charcoal ash on my compost pile?

Fireplace ash is fine, as long as you have not burned plastics, painted wood or treated wood in the fire. (And this is something you should avoid doing anyway.) Charcoal ash, on the other hand, should not be added to the compost pile.

Can I compost grass clippings sprayed with weed killer?

Recent research suggests that the compost process may neutralize certain toxins. However, this depends, among other things, on the chemical composition of the toxin, the temperature reached in the compost process and whether or not the chemical is water-soluble. It makes more sense to leave the clippings on the lawn (which may help your grass get so healthy that you don't have to apply herbicides any more).

What are the composting options for apartment dwellers?

If you live in an apartment that does not have a balcony, you can either compost indoors with worms or get together with people in your building to ask the landlord if you can set up a compost bin outside on the apartment grounds.

On a balcony, you can compost with a garbage can and air

stack (see Chapter 3); with a rotating drum composter; or with a balcony-sized holding unit.

Will worms in vermicomposting bins try to escape?

No! We have never heard of this happening. Worms *love* their worm bin homes and have no reason to leave. If you're really worried about this, you can put nylon mesh on the inside of your vermicomposter.

Will my compost pile smell bad?

Compost piles only smell bad when something is going wrong. Bad odours usually mean that the compost is not getting enough air. You can fix this by turning the pile or aerating it in some other way, like fluffing materials and poking air holes with a broom handle. If you then add a layer of soil, it will absorb the odours.

Will my compost pile attract animals?

If you're not adding meat, bones, fish or dairy products to your pile, and if you're careful about burying all food waste under a layer of soil, then animals should not be a problem. However, the best way to pest-proof your pile is to enclose it completely with heavy gauge, ¼" or ½" hardware cloth.

How can I get rid of flies around my compost pile or vermicomposter?

Bury your food waste additions to the pile or vermicomposter under soil.

Where's the motor?

It's nice to know that in our mechanized, industrialized society, there are still some things that happen naturally — compost bins do not have motors!

■ 8 ■

Soil and Garden Gold: Using Compost

Soil. Can you think of a substance that has had more meaning for humanity? ... most of the world's people are tillers of the soil and, in a very real sense, the soil is their source of life.
— Henry D. Foth, *Fundamentals of Soil Science*

The complex community of organisms in soil, the reactions and balances and changes that occur, make the micro-community of your compost pile look relatively simple by comparison. Soil is the foundation on which a living, healthy garden depends; you can plant the best seeds, weed them faithfully, water them religiously, talk to them end-lessly, but if you don't have good soil, your efforts will be in vain. This is why organic gardeners and those involved in ecological agriculture make soil health their first priority: they feed the soil instead of providing quick-fix, "conve-nience" foods for plants.

The quantity and the composition of organic matter and nutrients are the most important features of your garden soil. Humus, of course, is the end product of composting.

Humus improves the soil's structure, increasing the soil's ability to absorb and retain moisture. Humus also makes the soil easier to cultivate. Most important, humus provides food for soil micro-organisms which in turn recycle minerals and nutrients for the growing plants. Thus, by adding humus (in

the form of finished compost) to your soil, you are improving the soil environment *and* providing the necessary ingredients for plant growth.

If you add compost regularly, you will eliminate the need
for quick-fix, synthetic fertilizers.

FOOD FOR THOUGHT

The manufacturing of synthetic nitrogen fertilizers requires a
great deal of energy, and energy consumption is exactly
what we have to cut down on. According to the United
Nations Environment Programme, North Americans use an
average of 9 lbs (4 kgs) of artificial fertilizer on a typical lawn
each year — 10 times more per acre than farmers use on
cropland — and over half is wasted, ending up in lakes and
streams where it causes damage.

Using compost and organic fertilizers instead, to revital-
ize your garden, makes good environmental sense.

ORGANIC FERTILIZER

| 1 part bloodmeal | 3 parts wood ash or peat moss |
| 2 parts bonemeal | 4 parts leaf mould or compost |

Source: Canadian Organic Growers

KNOW YOUR SOIL

Soil structure refers to how inorganic particles (of sand, silt
and clay) and humus are bound together. Soil with a good
structure is easy to turn over, but it is not so light that it won't
hold together. It drains well, but retains some moisture.

Soil consists primarily of sand, silt and clay. Sand particles
are the largest; clay particles, the smallest. These inorganic
particles combine with organic material, in different propor-
tions, to produce topsoil.

Sandy Soil:

Looks loose, friable, no large particles. Won't hold its shape when you squeeze it in your hand. Does not retain water and nutrients.

Clay Soil:
Looks hard, compact, no pores or spaces to hold air or water. Forms lumps when you squeeze it. Gets very sticky when wet; turns very hard when dry.

Silt Soil:
Combines characteristics of both sandy and clay soil.

Loam:
Looks porous, has particles or crumbs of different sizes. Forms into a ball when you squeeze it, but will break apart easily. Holds water. It's a mixture of humus, clay, sand and silt.

FINISHED COMPOST: WHEN IT'S READY
In a letter to the *Toronto Star* (March 19, 1991), the following description appeared: "The faint fragrance of finished compost has often been compared to the odour we would perceive on scuffling the forest floor after a rain — in other words an odour of rare freshness and vitality in our paved-over world."

This lush and elegant description perfectly describes the smell of finished compost, but you'll have to use more than your nose to determine when your compost is done, though the nose is good guide. If, for example, the material smells mouldy or rotten, it's not ready and the pile probably needs more air.

Let's assume that you have been caring for your pile for four months. You've put a balance of "greens" and "browns" into the heap, poked air holes for ventilation, monitored the moisture level and now you think that you may have some finished compost in the bottom layer.

Take some of the compost out for inspection. Is it crumbly

and moist? or stringy and dry? Can you identify any of the original materials? or is it uniformly dark and soil-like? Does it smell "fresh"? Can you see any tiny bugs crawling around in it?

When compost is ready it should be dark, crumbly and fresh smelling. It should resemble soil. Most of the original materials should not be recognizable, though things that take a long time to decompose (egg shells, cherry pits, nut shells, twigs, for example) will probably still be visible. But don't worry, these things can be screened out, put back on the pile, and the rest of the compost used. Stringy bits of material can usually be crushed with your hand.

If you have a soil thermometer, you can take the pile's temperature: if it's much warmer than the surrounding air, then the compost is still working and it needs more decomposition time.

SIGNS OF "DONENESS"

- Crumbly, loose structure: not in clumps or lumpy.
- Dark brown in colour.
- Earthlike smell.

COMPOST FOR SOIL CONDITIONING

Midge Ellis Keeble, the author of *Tottering in My Garden*, has a wonderfully luscious way of describing the difference between compost and good garden soil: "Topsoil and compost are not quite the same. One is chocolate cake and the other is devil's food cake or Black Forest cake, all depending on just how wickedly rich you make it."

Your finished compost may or may not be, technically, a fertilizer, depending on the nutrient content of the finished batch. However, organic gardeners maintain soil fertility by using compost. Instead of providing instant food for plants (as soluble fertilizers do), compost builds up the organic matter of soil, providing a constant store of nutrients that are available to plants as they need them. At Rodale Press (the publishers of *Organic Gardening* magazine), they call this the "soil bank account" theory. The purpose is to build permanent fertility into the soil by adding to its mineral reserves and humus content. As well, compost adds bacteria and micro-organisms to the soil, which keep it alive, active and changing.

In compost that is ready, the degradable organic matter has turned into humus. If you're not sure that your compost is done, it's better to leave it to decompose some more rather than putting it on the garden too early. If incorporated into the soil while compost is still actively decomposing, it will temporarily rob the soil of its nitrogen, which the plants would be happier using. However, if you add partially decomposed material to the soil in the fall, the composting process will continue over winter and the nutrients will be available to plants in time for spring gardening. Of course, the flip side is that if you store compost for too long, some of its nutrients may leach away. (Stored compost should be covered with a plastic sheet, to reduce leaching.)

BENEFITS OF COMPOST TO SOIL

- Improves soil texture.
- Improves soil's water-retention capability.
- Improves soil's aeration capacity.
- Improves soil's resistance to erosion.
- Helps keep soil temperature stable.
- Adds and stores nutrients in the soil.
- Improves soil's ability to absorb rapid changes in acidity and alkalinity.
- May neutralize certain toxins.

WHEN TO USE COMPOST
Although you can apply compost to your garden whenever the compost is ready, to get the maximum value from its nutrients the best time to apply compost is about a month

before planting in the spring. If the ground can be dug, the compost should be worked into the soil thoroughly, to a depth of approximately four to six inches. Spring soils that have had compost applied will generally hold their heat and moisture better than plain soil.

However, compost can also be dug into the soil in the fall. The advantage of fall application is that you can use compost that isn't completely ready. It will continue working in the

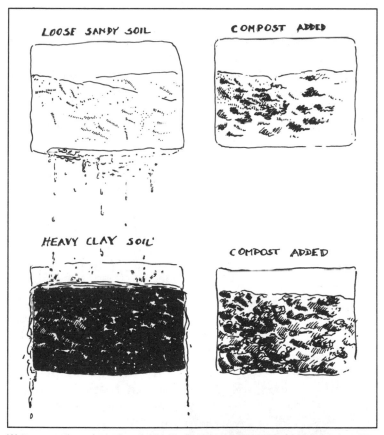

Water seeps through sandy soils quickly. But when compost is added, the water retention ability of sandy soil is increased. Clay soil gets water-logged quickly and sheds excess water; again, when compost is added the water-retention ability of clay soil is increased.

soil and be ready to supply nutrients by the spring. As well, it may be easier to work the soil in the fall than in the spring.

You can store compost if it's ready in the fall but you don't want to use it until spring. However, to discourage nutrient leaching, cover the heap with plastic or some kind of tarpaulin.

If your compost is ready in the summer, you can either apply it as a top dressing, dig it in as a side dressing around your plants, or wait until fall for a thorough working in.

COMPOST AND SOIL

You can never add too much compost to your garden. Unlike commercial fertilizers, which may burn plants, the nutrients in compost are released slowly and continuously. Sandy soils, in particular, benefit greatly from lots of compost, which builds up organic matter and helps hold nutrients.

For both sandy and clay soils, compost improves both their texture and their water-retaining ability, and makes it easier for roots to take hold.

Mulch can extend your growing/harvesting season.

COMPOST APPLICATIONS

Gardeners rarely ask, "How much compost should I use?" This is because you can never add too much compost to your soil. However, if you want some kind of guideline, figure on about 20 bushels of compost for a garden that's 100 square feet — every year!

Garden:

If you have enough compost, try to add at least half

an inch to the whole garden every year — or, one to two pounds of compost for every two square feet of soil. Mix it into the soil thoroughly, to a depth of approximately four inches.

If you don't have enough to treat the whole garden, dig compost into the spots where you plan to put your heaviest, neediest feeders (for example, corn, tomatoes, fruit trees, roses). Although best done either in spring or in fall, you can add compost throughout the growing season.

Vegetable Garden:

When you're digging your trenches either for seeds or seedlings, put a handful of compost in the furrows for each plant. Then, while the plant is growing, you can add compost as a top dressing or mulch.

Here's an idea for gardeners who want to start plants early, indoors. In the fall, take a bucketful of finished compost and store it in the basement. If you're worried about bugs, sterilize the compost in the oven at 180° F (80° C) for half an hour (it will smell very pungent). Then, when you need compost for starting seeds inside in the late winter, you won't have to chip away at a frozen heap.

Flower Garden:

For annuals, compost can be applied when planting either seeds or seedlings. Again, put a handful of compost in the hole for each plant.

For perennials, compost can be applied around the plants and either dug in or left as a mulch.

Lawn:

For new lawns, work in as much compost as you have, digging to a depth of six inches. For established lawns that are patchy in places, work compost in bare spots, soak with water and plant grass seed.

To feed your lawn, finely screened compost makes an excellent top dressing.

Trees and Shrubs:

When planting new trees or shrubs, make a hole about twice the size of the root ball. Fill the hole around the plant with a mixture (equal parts) of compost, good sandy topsoil and peat moss. Stamp down and soak thoroughly. Apply a few inches of compost on top of the soil. For growing trees and shrubs, apply compost as a top dressing from the trunk out to the drip line (ends of the branches). Work about one to two inches of compost into the soil.

Houseplants:

All of the nutrients for your houseplants have to come from the soil in the pot, which can get depleted of nutrients and compacted, so regular additions of compost help to return the soil to fertility. An inch of two of compost worked into the soil two or three times a year is a good idea. Even more feedings can be given if plants show signs of unhealthiness, such as yellowing leaves, wilting, or dropping of leaves.

Homemade compost tea barrel.

Compost is very useful when you're potting houseplants. Mix equal parts sterilized loam or top soil, peat moss or sand, and compost. Use as you would any regular potting soil.

COMPOST TEA, ANYONE?

Brew up a batch of this elixir for watering your plants. The nutrients in the compost dissolve into the water, which can then be applied directly to your plants. This **compost tea** is especially good for unhealthy plants, giving them a quick fix.

For a simple recipe, put equal parts of compost and water into a bucket or watering can. Stir a few times and leave for a day or so. Use the water for your neediest plants.

You can use the same compost to make a few batches of compost tea, as not all the nutrients will be used up in one "go." After you've used the same compost a few times, dig it into the garden (or put it back on the compost pile) and use fresh compost for more tea. (There will still be some nutrients in the spent compost — some nutrients are not water soluble — so it will still contribute nutrients to the soil.)

A more elaborate method of making compost tea is to fill a burlap bag or old pillow-case with compost. Place it in an old metal barrel or garbage can, hooking the bag onto the side if you can. Fill the can with water. Stir once a day. After a week the tea will be ready to use on houseplants or the garden. Some people even insert a tap near the bottom of the can for easy pouring of the tea (like juice-jugs on a picnic).

Another nutrient-rich plant food can be made using the same method but with composted manure instead of compost.

Compost tea makers are available commercially. An 8-gallon plastic unit (20" high x 13" wide x 15" deep) with spigot and reusable net "tea bag" is sold by mail order from Plow & Hearth (see Sources).

FOOD FOR THOUGHT

Your "rainbarrel" full of compost or manure tea, if uncovered, will be a great breeding ground for mosquitoes unless you put a goldfish or two in it to consume the larvae. A *very* happy goldfish.

SCREENING COMPOST

If you're using compost as a top dressing, it's best to sift the compost first, to get it into very fine pieces and to trap anything that is not completely decomposed.

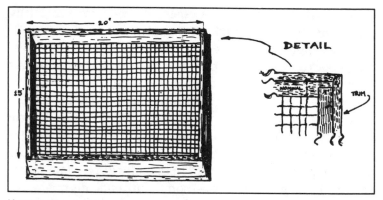

Homemade compost screen.

A fine screen (1/4" mesh) is good if you're using the compost in seed-starter pots. A bigger mesh (1/2") can be used for top dressing applications. Place the screen over an empty wheelbarrow or box and then sift the compost into this collector. Large pieces of undecomposed materials that separate out can go back onto the compost heap.

The Recycling Council of Ontario has drawn up the following plans for a 15"x20" screen that you can make yourself.

Materials:
- one 1"x3"x72" strapping or scrap lumber pieces
- 2' of 1/4" galvanized mesh (you can also use 1/2" mesh if you don't need such finely screened compost)
- carpenter's glue
- nails
- one 72" quarter-round trim
- staples

Construction:
Cut the 1x3 into four pieces, two at 20" and two at 15". Cut a 1/2" deep and 1" wide (or the width of your strapping) piece out of the two 15" ends. Use a handsaw and chisel to cut out these four lap cuts. Make a square frame, fitting the 20" sides into the 15" lap joints. Apply enough carpenter's

glue to hold it together, then nail it. Cut the galvanized mesh to the size of your square and staple it to the frame, or staple your mesh to the frame and then trim the edges with tinsnips. Tighten the tension of the galvanized mesh so it will not sag when filled with compost. Once the mesh is secure on the bottom of the frame, nail the quarter-round or 2" strapping over the mesh so it will hold the mesh in place and cover the mesh ends to prevent them from stabbing fingers and hands.

If you want to sift out undecomposed material from your compost but don't want to make your own sifter, you can buy a garden sieve (3/8" mesh or 1/4" mesh) from a gardening store or by mail order (see Sources). Kitchen collanders work well, too.

COMPOST CONCOCTIONS FOR SPECIAL PLANTS
This is where composting really begins to resemble cooking. You can make special compost "meals" for plants that have particular needs. For example, strawberries thrive in acidic conditions, so they respond well to compost that has been made using conifer needles (themselves highly acidic). The adventurous composter can experiment with matching plant needs with special compost concoctions.

Conifer Needle Compost:
Alternate needles from conifers (evergreens) with layers of food scraps and small amounts of manure. It may take a long time to break down into compost but when finished, you'll have a good compost for acid-loving plants such as rhododendrons, azaleas, strawberries, etc.

Leguminous Compost:
Use dead pea vines, bean or lupin plants, mixed with soil and a bit of lime to make a nitrogen-rich compost for use on leafy vegetable plants such as spinach or on brassicas (cauliflower, broccoli, etc.).

Straw Compost:
Use well-watered straw and manure to make a good top dressing for vegetables just before ripening. This compost dries out very easily, so check it often to keep it moist.

Tomato Compost:
Apparently tomatoes do well in compost made from dead tomato stalks (cannibal tomatoes?). It's fine to apply this compost before it's completely decayed.

COMPOST AS MULCHING MATERIAL
To use compost as a mulch, just place a few inches of it on top of the soil around plants during the growing season or over the whole garden in the spring and fall.

You can also try growing a "living mulch" between rows of annuals or vegetables. Called cover crops or green manures, low-growing "living mulches" such as clover add nitrogen to the soil and provide an attractive carpet. Plant them from seed in the spring, then turn them under the soil in fall; decomposition will occur over the winter and in spring you'll have a particularly fertile bed for planting. (Chapter 2 has more information on cover crops and green manures.)

As you can see, compost can be used in many different ways. It really is gold for your garden. If you do end up with too much compost (unlikely as it may seem), you can always give it away. After all, gardening centres sell it by the truckload!

FOOD FOR THOUGHT

"In most parts of the world there is more life beneath the surface of the earth than above it ... Even in a teaspoon of soil there can be as many as ten million bacteria and two kilometres of fungal filaments."
— Stuart B. Hill, *Seasons* (Winter 1989)

■ 9 ■

Working Worms:
The Wonders of Wigglers

Some people may need years of therapy to get beyond
their fear of long, slimy, snake-like things. Once you
learn to appreciate worms (you don't really have to love
'em), your garden will be happier. Even better, worm
culture is the easiest way I know to recycle kitchen
scraps.
— Robert Kourik, *Garbage* (Nov/Dec 1989)

For the more adventurous, or for those who relish the idea of
sharing space with somewhat unconventional pets, you can
compost organic waste using worms. It's called **vermicomposting** — and the "verms" make very efficient composting
machines indeed.

"Vermi" comes from *vermis* — Latin for "worm" — so
vermicomposting is not for the squeamish. You'll be housing
at least 1,000 of these wigglers. However, if it's done properly, there are several advantages to worm composting:

- No smell (other than that of sweet-smelling compost).
- Doesn't take up much room (a small box the size of a
  "Blue Box" or recycling bin is all that's required).
- Noiseless (you can't hear them chomping!).
- They don't try to escape (your bin is worm heaven to
  them).
- They require little maintenance (you can take a vacation
  for days or a couple of weeks and they'll be fine).

Vermicomposting is ideal for people in apartments, or for composting at the office, or for people who don't like making the trip outdoors in winter to the backyard bin or heap. The major limitation of vermicomposting is that the system really can't handle garden wastes, unless the bin is very large. Worm composting is really only for kitchen waste.

However, the big advantage of vermicomposting is that it can be done indoors for the whole year, or outdoors for the warm months and then indoors for the winter.

WORM CITY

Where is Worm City, U.S.A.? According to Carl Woestendiek, Waste Reduction Planner for Seattle's Solid Waste Utility, "Seattle probably has the highest number of worm bins per capita of any city in the country." (*BioCycle*, May 1991). In Kalamazoo, Michigan—home of vermicomposter suppliers Flowerfield Enterprises—worms are eating the garbage of approximately 2,000 households.

Vermicomposting is like regular composting, except that you're using micro-organisms *and* a community of worms to break down organic matter. The advantage of adding worms to the composting process is that they're fast and they excrete a nutrient-rich manure (called castings), which is great for plants. According to Lady E.B. Balfour, "Worm casts contain five times more nitrogen, seven times more available phosphate, eleven times more potash, and 40 percent more humus than is normally to be found in the top six inches of soil, and this is not their only contribution to soil fertility" (*The Living Soil*).

The vermicomposting process works by placing worms in a bin or container that has been prepared with a bedding material. Kitchen wastes are added as they become available and are dug into the bedding. The worms immediately get to work, chomping through the material — some eat their own weight in food every day — and excreting castings, the main ingredient of vermicompost. Eventually, you will accumulate enough compost or castings to harvest. As well, since the worms continue to reproduce, you have the option of harvesting them (giving them to friends to start their own worm bins, taking them to the office, or starting a second bin in your home) or letting the worm population stabilize naturally.

WORM ECOLOGY

Before getting into the details of vermicomposting, it may help to know a little about worms, their physical make-up and their habits. Like nature's ploughs, worms move through the earth and provide aeration for the soil and tunnels for plant roots and drainage. They keep the earth in a constant natural boil, so to speak. As well, they recycle nutrients through their bodies, literally grinding their way through matter, excreting nutrient-rich castings.

Worms "breathe" (respire) by absorbing oxygen through the surface of their bodies and sending out carbon dioxide. Although different species have different minimum oxygen requirements, all worms need oxygen to survive. They also require fairly moist environments because a worm's body is from 75 to 90 percent water by weight.

FOOD FOR THOUGHT

The worms in your garden are unacknowledged heroes. The more, the better, and here's why. Worms:
- Aerate the soil; they bring in oxygen, by tunnelling.
- Improve moisture retention in soil.
- Create tunnels for roots to grow in easily.
- Convert organic matter into nutrients for plants.
- Bring surface litter down into the soil, an important role in the breakdown of material.
- Enhance microbial activity by consuming organic matter, mixing it with soil and excreting nutrients.

Worms eat organic matter: plants (decaying and fresh), protozoans, rotifers, nematodes, bacteria, fungi, decomposing remains of other animals, and bits of soil.

Worms are valuable in the soil not just for their tunnelling, which improves soil texture, but also for what they excrete: castings. These castings are made up of brokendown organic matter and minerals from the soil, and they are excellent soil conditioners.

Worms reproduce either biparentally, in which case genetic material is exchanged with another worm of the same species (as occurs in dew worms and manure worms), or uniparentally, in which no cross-fertilization occurs. In this case, one worm produces the ovum and releases it as a cocoon. Each cocoon that is created produces one or two worms (although in manure worms, it may be over ten worms). These worms reach reproductive maturity in three weeks to a year, and once sexually mature, they can produce two to three cocoons a week for six months to a year. In biparental fertilization, both worms have male and female organs, and they cross-fertilize simultaneously. Red wigglers can produce up to 240 offspring in a six-month period, providing they are happy. In other words, worms are prolific. Or, as Anna Draper of Early Bird Ecology and Bait Farms puts it: "Romance is never a problem for the redworm. A true hermaphrodite, every earthworm has both male and female sex organs. So if it's not near the one it loves, it loves the one it's near." (Even itself.)

One interesting feature of worms is that some species are able to regenerate amputated segments of their bodies: a tail won't grow a new head but a head might grow a new tail. The fact that they are so hardy is a comfort, particularly when you start handling the worms at harvest time, and accidentally cut through the odd one.

WORM VARIETIES

Different worm species have different requirements. In

vermicomposting, you don't use regular earthworms from the garden because they don't reproduce well in captivity and can't take the heat. Instead, you use the following worm varieties:

Manure or Redworm (Eisenia foetida):

Also known as red wiggler because of its spunky nature, this worm is commonly found in manure piles, rotting leaf piles and compost piles in North America. It reproduces well in temperatures between 68-77° F (20-25° C), but can't survive in an outside bin in winter unless it has insulation. Red wigglers work best in an indoor bin, thrive in high-density conditions, and reproduce well in captivity. (If conditions are favourable, the population can double or triple in just a few months.) This fast worker rapidly decomposes organic materials.

When mature, the worm is up to 3" to 4" in length, though it stays fairly thin. Its shiny skin has a reddish tinge, and although it does not have eyes, it hates bright light.

Redworms are easy to buy commercially, but you can also find them in manure piles, leaf piles or ready-to-harvest compost.

African Night Crawler (Endrilus eugeniae):

This is another kind of worm sold for composting. It can tolerate temperatures ranging from 68-80° F (20-26° C), but the optimum is about 75° F (24° C). It can't survive below 60° F (15° C), and growth and reproductive rates drop below 68° F (20° C).

There's a list of places that sell vermicomposting worms in the Sources section at the back of this book.

STARTING OUT

Vermicomposting in most of North America is done indoors because composting worms need relatively warm temperatures. You can put them outside in the summer (or year-round if you live in southern states), but you'll have less control over moisture and heat.

Indoors, you'll need a place to keep the worm bin. It takes up approximately 1'x2'x3', so you need an out-of-the-way place. Make sure that it's in a convenient enough location to get to for additions of food scraps (and also where visitors — who will most likely want to see it — can get to it). A basement is where many people choose to put their bins, because it is usually dark, which the worms love. However, make sure it's in a place where there's no danger of flooding. Although we've never actually heard of a cat-worm catastrophe, we suspect that there may be some curious felines out there who just might use an uncovered worm bin as a cat tray. So, you might want to keep the bin off the ground.

Places that could be too hot include heated attics, outside under the hot sun, or elevated in a greenhouse. Good storage places include corners, cupboards, under a table, or at the top of the stairs. Some people give their bins a position of prominence, like a conversation piece. The Seattle Tilth Association (see Sources) produces design plans for a lidded worm bin that is sturdy enough to double as a piece of patio furniture! For convenience, you can't beat the bin described by Mary Appelhof in her excellent book *Worms Eat My Garbage*: "One of my friends has a worm bin on top of his dishwasher with a cutting board serving for a lid. When he is through chopping cabbage, celery or whatever, he just slides the top back and scrapes the waste into his worm bin."

RULE OF THUMB

If you're keeping your worms outside on the balcony, bring them in when the temperature drops below 40° F (5° C).

Once you have decided where your bin will go, you need to determine the exact size of bin that's appropriate for you. The container should be shallow, approximately 8" to 12" deep, because if it is deeper, the bottom layers of material could become anaerobic and smelly. The greater the surface area of the bin, in general, the better the aeration. Also, with a greater surface area, there's more room to rotate the food scraps you add. How large it is depends on how much kitchen waste your household produces, although there are a few guidelines. A good rule of thumb is to have one square foot of surface area per pound of weekly garbage. In other words, a 2'x3' bin, 1' deep, would be appropriate for a household that produces 6 lbs of food waste a week. You may want to weigh your garbage for a week to determine the appropriate size.

VARIABLES IN VERMICOMPOSTING
The variables that affect the success of worm composting are very similar to the variables that affect other composting methods: the size of the container; the health of the worms; temperature inside and outside the bin; moisture level inside the bin; pH of food scraps; appropriateness of the bedding material; and the nature of food scraps added to the bin.

Worms' Needs
- **Proper temperature:** the best range is 65-77° F (20-25° C)
- **Adequate moisture and suitable drainage:** worms need to keep moist in order to breathe through their skins, but they are suffocated by too much moisture
- **Ventilation:** worms need oxygen, so there should be free circulation of air around your bin
- **Food:** your food wastes make great worm food, but they should always be covered with the bedding material to discourage fruit flies
- **Proper pH:** worms prefer a neutral pH (approximately 7); if their environment gets too acidic (pH below 5.5), they may die off; balance any additions of acidic food wastes such as citrus peels with pulverized egg shells

WORM BINS

As with regular composting, there is enormous variety in the type of bin you can use: a wooden, plastic, or metal container, or a commercially available vermicomposter. The most important thing is that the bin should not be too deep (8″ to 12″ is ideal) and there should be aeration holes for ventilation. If you choose a container that has been used for something else, make sure that it wasn't used to store pesticides, herbicides or other chemicals.

If you're building your own bin, 1' high x 2' wide x 3' long should be adequate for 6 lbs of garbage a week (this is the average amount of food waste from 4 to 6 people). Plywood is fine (3/8" exterior grade, because the bin will get wet), though make sure it hasn't been treated (pressure-treated wood may have a greenish tinge). Also, avoid a highly aromatic wood such as cedar or redwood because some worms don't like it. The bottom piece for the bin will be 2'x3', attached to the sides with nails or screws. Drill ten to twenty holes in the bottom piece (1/2" bit is fine), and place up on blocks with a piece of sheet plastic underneath. If you're worried about worms or bits of compost escaping through the ventilation holes, you can put a piece of fine nylon mesh (or pantyhose) as a lining inside or try using a few sheets of newspaper on the bottom and sides. A lid is optional; if you don't want to make a lid, you can just use a sheet of dark plastic on top.

> **Will the worms try to escape? No — worms are shy creatures who love the dark. They'll stay put as long as you feed them good stuff.**

1-2-3 Vermicomposting Bin — Adapted from and reproduced by permission of the Seattle Engineering Department's Solid Waste Utility and the Seattle Tilth Association.

Can handle approximately six pounds of food waste each week — roughly that produced by a family of four to six.

Materials:
- one 4'x8' sheet of 1/2" plywood
- one 12' 2"x4"
- one 16' 2"x4"
- 1 lb 2" galvanized nails
- 1/2 lb 3-1/2" galvanized nails
- two galvanized door hinges
- non-toxic wood preservative

Construction:
Measure and cut the plywood as per drawing.

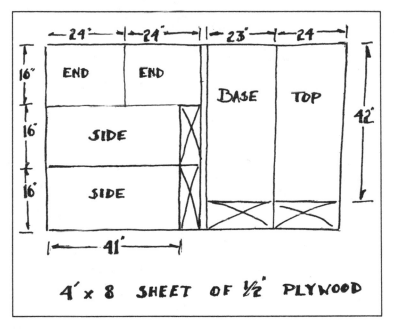

Cut the 12' 2x4 into five pieces: two 39", two 23" and one 20". Nail these 2x4s together on edge with two 3-1/2" nails at each joint as illustrated in the Base Frame detail (page 126). Nail the plywood base piece onto the 2"x4" frame. Cut four 1' lengths out of the 16'x2"x4". Nail a 1'x2"x4" onto each end of the side panels flush with the top and side edges of the plywood. Nail the side pieces onto the base frame.

To complete the box, nail the ends onto the base and sides. Drill twenty 1/2" holes through the bottom of the box for drainage and aeration.

To make the lid, take the remaining 12'x2"x4" and cut it into two 45" pieces and two 20" pieces and lay them flat — so that the plywood top is inset from the edges of the 2x4 by 1-1/2" all around the perimeter. Nail the plywood onto the 2x4s. Attach hinges to the backside of the box at both ends of the 2x4s, and on the underside of the lid frame.

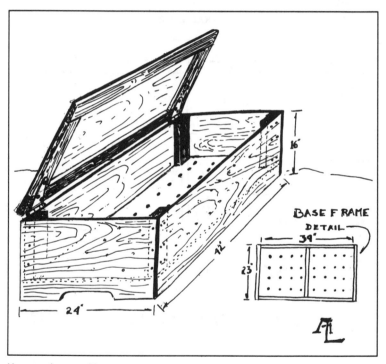

Homemade worm bin.

Small-scale Vermicomposter

This bin will handle approximately four pounds of food waste per week — or roughly that produced by one or two people.

Materials:
- one 4'x8' sheet of 1/2" plywood
- 36 — 2" galvanized nails
- non-toxic wood preservative

Construction:
Cut four pieces of plywood 23-1/2"x8" for the sides. Nail them together, overlapping at the corners. Cut one piece of plywood 24"x24" for the bottom. Secure the bottom to the sides using about five nails per side. Drill twelve 1/2" holes in the bottom for aeration and drainage. Use a dark plastic sheet as a cover.

An unfinished wood box will last a few years. You can extend the bin's life by using a non-toxic wood varnish. Although wood is better than plastic in terms of absorbing moisture and "breathing," wooden bins may start to smell a bit, whereas plastic won't. Some people prefer using plastic bins because they are easier to clean and often weigh less than wood. Local moving companies may sell their plastic bins; you'll have to drill holes in the top and bottom and place on blocks to allow air circulation. A rubber mat underneath will catch any liquid run-off.

RULE OF THUMB

With worm bins, deeper isn't necessarily better. The container should be fairly shallow (8"-12") because:
- Redworms tend to be surface feeders.
- Bedding will get matted in a deep container, causing smelly anaerobic conditions.
- Bins with larger surface area rather than greater depth have more room for adding and mixing food waste.

COMMERCIAL WORM BINS
You can buy commercial worm bins. For example, the American Horticultural Society (see Sources) distributes a worm bin that will process food waste from two or three

adults, and is made of high-density, dark green plastic. Flowerfield Enterprises (see Sources), pioneers of vermicomposting, also sells a bin called the Work-a-way, which comes in two sizes; included is Mary Appelhof's informative *Worms Eat My Garbage.*

Canadian Original Vermicomposter has started manufacturing an insulated worm bin that can be used outdoors throughout the winter. The bin comes in different sizes; the largest is 3' x 3'.

Check at a gardening centre or environmental products store for commercial bins, or call a local environment group or recycling group to see if they know of any worm bin sources.

BEDDING

Good bedding holds moisture, allows for air circulation, and gives the worms a damp place to live and work (and you a good place to bury your garbage). The bedding can be made out of a number of different materials, although it must be a natural material because worms eat the bedding along with your food waste. Another important feature of the bedding is that it has to be porous so that it enhances air movement, but compact enough so that it will hold water. (If you try to compost food without the bedding, you will probably produce a slimy, smelly mess.)

Shredded newspapers make good bedding, mixed with soil, though you should avoid coloured newspapers because some of the inks may contain heavy metals, which are bad for the worms and the garden. Immerse the paper in water for a few minutes, then wring out and cut into 1"-2" wide strips. If the strips seem to be compacting when you put them in the bin, try to fluff them up.

You can also use corrugated cardboard; like newspapers, immerse in water, wring out and shred or cut into strips. Peat moss can also be used (you'll have to add water — and some crushed egg shells to counter the acidity).

Put a layer of approximately 3" to 4" of bedding into the worm bin or until it is half full. Then add a 2" layer of soil, dead leaves, straw, peat moss or any mixture of these materials. (Make sure that no pesticides or herbicides have contaminated the soil, leaves or grass. Worms are very sensitive to toxic chemicals.) Sprinkle or spray water until the bedding is damp but not dripping. The bedding should be as moist as a wrung-out sponge. Worms are more than 75 percent water, and the bedding should match this. (Once you get started, the food wastes should keep the bin moist enough for the worms.)

Bedding Materials

Straw:
Straw takes a long time to break down but it does provide a good bedding structure. Should be mixed with another bedding material such as peat moss.

Peat Moss:
Soak it in water overnight to reduce its acidity, then squeeze before using. Because peat moss is acidic, you should add crushed egg shells to neutralize the acid.

Leaves:
Don't use leaves if you're worried about bringing outdoor bugs inside. Leaves should be shredded first. Best used if mixed with another material because leaves alone tend to mat, keeping out necessary air. Make sure that leaves have not been sprayed and that they have not been contaminated by heavy metals near roadways.

Corrugated Cardboard and Paper:
Soak and shred before using. Best used if mixed with other materials, such as peat moss which is fluffy, to prevent compaction. Don't use waxed, bleached, coloured or white cardboard, coloured comics or coated (glossy) paper.

Soil:
Easy to find and cheap to use as bedding. Best mixed with other bedding materials that worms will eat, such as leaves.

Some people don't use garden soil to avoid importing bugs. Don't use hard clay soils.

BRING ON THE WORMS

When you have the bin and bedding prepared, it's time for the worms. Redworms (a.k.a. red wigglers) and African night crawlers are the worms of choice. They are available from fishing or bait stores, and gardening centres. (If you're buying them from a bait supplier, make sure that they are in fact redworms or African night crawlers and not dew worms.) If you can't find a worm source in your area, contact a local recycling group, a local agriculture college, an environmental store or mail-order company, or check organic gardening or fishing magazines. Most commercial worm growers will ship through the mail, and worms are available year round. If you want to scavenge, you can get redworms from digging around in a manure pile or a rotting leaf pile — their natural habitat — but make sure you're not taking earthworms as well, because they will die in your vermicomposter. (See Sources at the end of the book for worm source addresses.)

How many worms you'll need depends on the size of bin and the amount of food waste you're throwing out per week. For the 1'x2'x3' box (which can handle 1 lb of food waste a day), use 2 lbs of worms. In other words, a ratio of 2:1 (worms:garbage) is appropriate. Note that worms are sold by the pound, not by the number of worms. There are approximately 1,000 worms per pound. (The cost will vary from source to source, but they're approximately $10-20 a pound.)

Don't worry about getting exactly the right number of worms the first time you set up your bin. The worm population will stabilize. If you don't put in enough at first, it will just take longer to process your waste. If you put in too many, on the other hand, the worms won't grow or reproduce as quickly and some may die.

Inelegant as it sounds, just plop the worms onto the bedding. Because they don't like light, they will quickly move below the surface. Any that don't move from the light after a while are probably dead and you can just leave them to decompose.

If your composter has a lid, close it after adding the worms. Or, put a sheet of dark plastic over the bin to keep light out and moisture in.

Now you're ready to start feeding your worms.

Number of People	Quantity of Worms	Bin Size
1-2	1 pound	1'x1.5'x2'
2-3	1 pound	1'x2'x2'
4-6	2-3 pounds	1'x2'x3.5'

WIGGLER FEEDING

Worms will thrive on any organic food waste. However, you should not feed them meat, bones and fish scraps because these will cause odour in the bin. And, as with any composting, non-biodegradable materials — non-organic materials that will not break down — should not be added. Some people also avoid cheese and oils, but if added in moderation, these should not be a problem. However, if the bin starts to smell, stop adding them.

Worms are very good at ploughing through almost anything. Even coffee filters and tea bags are okay. Egg shells should be pulverized completely because the worms find them hard and brittle.

A feeding chart on the lid will help remind you to rotate food wastes you add to the vermicomposter.

Food scraps should be buried completely under the bedding to keep the bin from smelling and to discourage fruit flies. Cover all additions with bedding. If you're adding your waste daily, then you can plan a rotation to avoid overloading one place in the bin. Those inclined to super-organization could put a chart or graph on the lid of their bin and mark the date and location of each addition of materials. Or, you can put a drinking straw or popsicle stick in the bedding to mark the place where you've just added food. However, worms, unlike other pets, do not require a regular feeding schedule!

You will speed up the process and reduce the chance of odour if you chop materials into fine pieces. Worms literally plough through their food, so the smaller the pieces, the better.

It's important not to overload the system with food waste. For example, if you're having lots of guests, you may want to add wastes gradually over the next few days, rather than all at once. (You can keep excess waste in the fridge, so it doesn't smell, or even in the freezer.) If you've added too much, you'll be able to tell with your nose. Stop adding food for a few days until the smell goes away. On the other hand, it is possible to underfeed worms too. If you go away for three weeks or more, the population may die off.

RULE OF THUMB

When using tap water for your worms, let it sit for 24 hours first so the chlorine evaporates.

You should also monitor the moisture level of your worm bin. Although it probably won't dry out if you're adding food regularly, you may have to sprinkle water on the dried-out sides. Sometimes potato bits or other vegetables will start to sprout in your bin; these steal moisture, so pull them out, chop them up and add to the bin again.

Do Feed Worms:
- Vegetable scraps, chopped into fine pieces
- Tea bags and loose tea
- Coffee grounds
- Pulverized egg shells
- Fruit and fruit rinds, chopped
- Bread and baked goods, chopped
- Rice and grains
- Nuts, chopped
- Pasta, chopped

Don't Feed Worms:
- Bones
- Fish
- Meat
- Butter
- Cheese
- Very oily food
- Yard waste

You can make your worms a special "milkshake" by putting your food scraps in a blender with a bit of water, pureeing and pouring the liquid into the bin. They love it!

Don't worry if citrus fruit scraps seem to take a long time to decompose — they can take as long as a month. Chop them into small pieces to speed things up.

Let your egg shells dry out, then crush them in a paper bag with a rolling pin, or with a mortar and pestle.

HARVESTING VERMICOMPOST

The length of time it takes to get finished compost varies from one worm bin to another, on the worm population and the food added. However, in anywhere from two to three months, you should notice that the volume of materials in your vermicomposter has dropped. Even though you are adding new food, the volume drops because the bedding is decomposing and being consumed by the worms. You'll also find it difficult to recognize the original bedding material and instead find many worm castings, which look like small, black pellets.

There are a number of different ways to harvest finished compost.

The One-Step Method:
Take off the lid. When exposed to light, the worms will dig down deeper. Scoop out a layer of compost, returning any

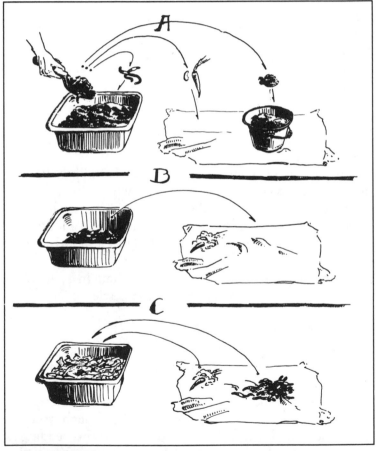

One-step harvesting of vermicompost. All vermicompost is taken out of the bin, new bedding is prepared and the worms are put back into the bin.

worms that come along with the scoop. If you can recognize food in the scoop, set the recognizable bits aside for later return to the prepared bin. Put scooped-out, finished compost into a container. Scoop out another layer, following the same procedure. Wait a few minutes to allow worms to dig down. Scoop out another layer. When you've taken out most of the finished compost, you should have a mass of wigglers at the bottom. Pour them onto a sheet of plastic and prepare new worm bedding for them (see original set-up). Return worms to their new bedding and also add any uncomposted food scraps that you salvaged in the process. The worms will now start vermicomposting all over again.

The Back-and-Forth Method:

When the original bedding is no longer recognizable, move all the compost and worms over to one side of the bin. Put new bedding (peat moss, shredded cardboard or newspaper) on the vacant side of the bin. Bury new food waste in the new bedding only and cover the new bedding side only with plastic or lid. The worms in the pile of finished compost (the old pile) will migrate over to the new bedding where the food is. After about two weeks, all of the worms should have moved over and you are ready to harvest the finished

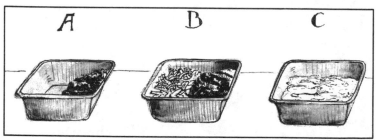

Back-and-forth harvesting of vermicompost. Vermicompost is moved to the right side of the bin, new bedding is put in the left half. The worms migrate to the new bedding and food waste is put only in the new bedding. After one or two weeks, you can take out the vermicompost on the right and spread the new bedding throughout the bin.

compost. Under bright lights, scoop out a handful of compost from the finished pile. There shouldn't be any worms in the scoop, but check and return any strays to the new bedding. When you've removed all the finished compost, you can either place new bedding in that spot or spread bedding from the other side of the bin.

The Pile-and-Sort Method:

This is a muckier, get-right-into-it way of harvesting. Pour the contents of the worm bin onto a plastic sheet or spread-out newspapers. (This can be done either inside or outside if it's not too cold.) Under bright lights, make small piles out of the contents of the bin. The worms will dig down to the bottom of these piles.

After a few minutes, you can start to scoop the finished compost off the top and sides of the piles. Don't scoop it all at once; do it in layers. As well, to minimize worm disruption, you can rotate from one pile to the next, taking a layer off one, then a layer off another pile, so that when you're back at the first pile the worms will have had enough time to migrate away from the light.

If you find any uncomposted material in the piles, put it aside to add to the new bedding. When you've removed

most of the finished compost, you'll be left with little piles of squirming (unhappy-at-being-disturbed) worms. Prepare new bedding in the bin and put the worms back into the bin, along with

Pile-and-sort harvesting.

any uncomposted materials.

Perfection Method:
If you don't want to go through the pile-and-sort routine and you want

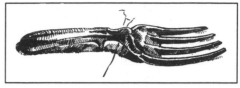

Use a garden fork to harvest your compost — you're less likely to hurt the worms than if you use a trowel.

absolutely finished, fine compost (with the other methods, you'll probably have to remove some uncomposted material from the castings), here is the perfectionist's method. Unfortunately, the worm population will die off with this method and you'll have to get new worms to set up the bin again. (This won't be a problem if you have access to a manure or leaf pile.)

With this method, you add food waste for approximately four months. Then you stop adding material and you let it just sit (and the worms work) for another three months or so. Of course, you'll want to compost your new food waste in another composting arrangement (or in a second worm bin) during the "working and waiting" period.

After approximately three months, the bin will be full of high-quality worm castings but very few worms (because no food is added, they die off). The finished compost will be ready to use.

FOOD FOR THOUGHT

At harvesting time, you may want to consider passing along some worms to a friend (or to a school) to start a vermicomposting unit. Even if you give away half the worms, your population will grow again once the worms are back in the bin and being fed. Or you can start your own second bin, stacking them one on top of the other. However, if you don't give any away, your worm population will stabilize itself and not overrun your bin.

This method is a good one for winter composting if you have an outside bin for use in the summer months. For example, you can set up the worm bin in the late fall when you no longer want to make the trip to your outdoor heap. Feed the worms scraps all winter, then let the bin sit all spring and into the summer. You will have finished compost to use in your summer garden, and then you can get more worms to set up the system again in the following late fall.

TROUBLESHOOTING
As with any other kind of composting, there are a number of problems that can arise if any one of the variables (moisture, ventilation, food material) is out of sync. Usually, it's easy enough to fix: you just have to recognize the problem and make an adjustment.

Fruit Flies and Fungus Gnats:
Unfortunately, your worm bin can become fruit-fly heaven. Just as fruit flies hang around bowls and baskets of fruit in the summer, they'll also flit around bins. The degree of infestation will depend on the amount of fruit you put into the bin (they hitchhike into bins on peels and rinds) and also the care you take in maintaining your bin. Fruit flies, while not actually bad for your compost, are a nuisance for you.

A trap will catch some fruit flies or you can use a vacuum cleaner.

One solution is to bury food waste into the bedding, rather than just placing it on top and sprinkling a bit of compost over it. You can also try freezing all fruit waste before adding it to the unit; first chop it into small pieces, freeze it for a few days and then let it thaw in the fridge before adding it to the worm bin. The freezing seems to kill the pests.

If you have an infestation, you may want to make a fruit fly trap. Put a few inches of beer in a glass. Poke a small hole (1/8" to 1/4") in a piece of plastic and place over the opening of the glass, securing the plastic with a rubber band. The fruit flies will head for the beer, get trapped inside and drown.

If the infestation is particularly bad, you can try vacuuming up the flies, if they seem to congregate in a few places. Throw out the vacuum cleaner bag immediately as they will reproduce in there. Fly paper may nab a few, too.

Since fruit flies and gnats are particularly a problem in the summer, you can move the bin outside, but don't put it in direct light. Find a cool, shady spot where pets can't get at it, and monitor the moisture level regularly (the bin will dry out faster outside).

Odour:

Under ideal conditions, your worm bin won't smell. But if you've overloaded it, either with water or with food, it may get a bit smelly. If it does, stop adding food waste, and after a week or so the smell should be gone.

The worms and micro-organisms doing the composting work need oxygen and a smelly bin is a sign of a lack of oxygen. If the bin smells and seems to be too wet, fluff up the materials and even turn the material over, so the lower stuff can dry out a bit.

Another cause of odour may be that the bin is too acidic, particularly if you've been adding lots of material such as tomatoes and citrus fruits. You can test the acidity using litmus paper or a soil testing kit (available at garden centres). Worms like a neutral to slightly acidic pH —

approximately 6-7 (7 is neutral; below 7 is increasingly acidic; above 7 is increasingly alkaline). You can counteract the acidity by adding powdered egg shells (a few tablespoons a week).

It's unlikely that your bin will be too wet if you're just adding food scraps and no extra water. But if the material seems wetter than a squeezed-out sponge, it may start to smell. You can either turn the materials to dry them out or add some extra bedding to soak up the excess moisture.

Water should never accumulate in the bottom of the bin. If your bin starts to smell, check for standing water, drain it and add more drainage holes to the bottom.

The other reason a bin might smell is because it is too deep (over 12") and the materials have compacted. This means that it's time to harvest some of the finished compost and prepare new bedding. You might want to consider having two bins if you generate a lot of food waste.

Grey Mould in Bin:

If a grey mould or fuzz appears on the surface of your worm bin, it is caused by overfeeding the worms. They aren't keeping up. Take the lid off, let the mould dry out and stop feeding the bin for a week.

Worm Die-Off

If your worm population is decreasing rather than increasing, it may be because the bin temperature is too high. Stop adding food scraps for a week (the heat is generated by micro-organisms decomposing food, not the worms). Die-off may also be caused by having too many worms for the space. Give some to a friend, start a second bin or put them in your outdoor compost pile in summer, if you have one. Worms will also die off if the bin is too wet (drain off excess water and aerate), too acidic (add powdered egg shells), or the bedding needs to be replaced.

Health Issues:
Worm bins do not reach high enough temperatures to kill pathogens, but this won't be a problem if you have not added meat or diseased materials. If you are sensitive to moulds, an indoor worm bin may cause problems.

Worm Predators:
If you're keeping your bin outdoors, be sure to use a lid because the following creatures find worms a tasty dish: birds, moles, hedgehogs, foxes, toads, snakes, beetles, leeches and slugs.

USING VERMICOMPOST
Many gardeners consider worm castings to be the most precious of all composts. The nutrient content is variable, depending on the food the worms are fed, but worm castings hold water extremely well and slowly release their nutrients into the soil. You can never use too much vermicompost on your plants.

Potting Soil:
Mix equal parts worm castings, sterilized soil, and sand or peat moss.

House Plants:
To fertilize house plants, add worm castings to soil and then water.

Garden:
Dig as many castings as you have into soil around vegetables, flowers, shrubs and trees. When transplanting seedlings, put a trowelful of castings into the soil. Evenly distribute in seed row when planting seeds.

Lawn:
You can use castings as top dressing to sprinkle over the lawn or you can rake into the grass. Or, when preparing a new lawn bed, put 1 part castings to 3 parts soil, spread seeds and water.

Note: Some plants, such as wildflowers, actually thrive in soil that is less fertile than rich soil, and don't particularly like being fertilized with worm castings. Save it for your needier plants like vegetables and roses.

Castings Tea:
Put 1 part worm castings and 3 parts water in a container, let it sit overnight. Stir and use to water plants.

Vermicomposting, because it's a relatively unusual activity (not for the worms, who have been doing it forever, but for householders, who are just starting to catch on), is a great educational tool. Friends and neighbours will want to hear more about it. Kids love it — 1,000 or more new pets! And many schools are starting to vermicompost in the classroom, as a way of teaching children about nature, the environment and reducing waste. (For more information about getting kids involved in vermicomposting, see Chapter 10.) You'll be spreading the environmental word about reducing waste and about recycling organic material back into the soil. So have fun doing this good work.

■ 10 ■

Composting with Kids

I can assure you that composting is a fascinating game
that grows on you.
— Lady E.B. Balfour, *The Living Soil*

Few things provide more hope for the future of this planet
than the fact that this generation of children is, in general,
keenly aware of environmental issues. And because it is
their future that is at stake, they are willing and enthusi-
astic about doing something to help the environment, to
solve the problems that we're now confronting. In many
instances, it's the young who are educating and mobilizing
their parents. The term "peer pressure" takes on an eco-
slant when kids with throw-away packaging (instead of
reusable containers) are ostracized in the school lunchroom.

Parents can go a long way towards developing their children's love for the environment — by teaching them about
composting and encouraging them with a number of compost activities. Through composting, kids learn about natural cyclical processes; they learn about different creatures in
the soil and about growth in the garden. Just as important,
they learn about garbage: how much they produce, what it's
made up of, how they might reduce it and how to recycle it.
Composting then becomes just one part of a larger environmental ethic that they are using to guide and inform all
activities in their lives.

Composting has a lot of things going for it as far as kids are concerned: it means they're not only allowed to, but they're actually encouraged to "play" with garbage! What could be more appealing?

THE FAMILY GARBAGE LOG

Keeping track of your trash is a good place to start environmental awareness, and to get children interested in composting and recycling. One way to do this is through a garbage log: a record sheet tacked on the refrigerator, for example, that serves as a garbage inventory.

THE GARBAGE LOG	M	T	W	T	F	S	S
Magazines							
Paper							
Packaging							
Food							
Yard Waste							
Cans							
Bottles							
Plastic containers							
Other							

Get everyone in the family to put an "x" beside each item you send to the landfill, a checkmark beside each item that you put in a "Blue Box" for recycling (if you have curbside recycling in your community), and a circle beside each item that can be composted. The goal, of course, is to have as few "x"s as possible and to keep everyone thinking about the make-up of your household garbage and just how much of it can be recycled.

If you want to get fancy, you can even keep a small scale in the kitchen for weighing the various components of your garbage. Prepare treats and prizes for those weeks in which you have more recyclable and compostable wastes kept out of the garbage than the material you throw out.

Classroom Log — For Teachers

This exercise provides a graphic example of just how quickly all that garbage adds up. Have each student calculate the amount of garbage his or her family probably throws out every day — based on the number of people in the household multiplied by an average of 2 kilograms (4.3 pounds) of garbage per person per day (U.S.) or 1.7 kilograms (3.5 pounds) of garbage per person per day (Canada). Collect each student's calculation and add them up for a classroom total.

room's height by its width, and that total by its length. Since an average of 222 kilograms of garbage occupies 1 cubic metre (14 pounds per cubic foot), and since you have both the weight of garbage produced by the class's families and the volume of the classroom, you can figure out how many days it would take to fill up the classroom with garbage.

KIDS' OWN COMPOST: A MICRO-PILE

It's easy to get kids interested in decomposition if they have their very own mini-pile to monitor — and they'll see just how quickly materials break down under the right conditions. They can build their compost piles in a big pickle jar (restaurant size) by adding layers of material, much like regular heap. For example, put a handful of dead leaves on the bottom, then a handful of garden soil, then a scoop of shredded kitchen waste, some more leaves, some grass clippings and more soil. Continue adding until the jar is full. If most of the materials are dry when they're "building" their micro-piles, add some water until the materials are as wet as a squeezed-out sponge. (They can also poke a small bundle of twigs through the materials, to serve as a ventilation stack.) They can experiment: put one in a sunny spot and one in shade; put one in a warm place and one in a cool place; have one dry, one damp, and one wet — and see whether there are any differences.

In a few days, the materials in an "ideal" place will start to settle and decompose — the students will probably be able to see changes in their micro-piles every day. In just a few weeks, most of the original materials will be unrecognizable and the kids will have finished compost — from their "best" bottles.

SCOUTING OUT A PROJECT

A Mississauga, Ontario Boy Scouts troop figured out a great way to raise money and to help the composting cause. The Scouts converted 2,000 plastic and metal drums (which they got free from companies that were happy not to have to send the drums to landfill) into composters by cutting off the ends of the drums and drilling holes in the sides. The Peel Region Public Works Department paid the Scouts $10 for each completed unit, which were then given away to households interested in starting to compost.

SCHOOL COMPOSTING

Kids are learning that there is more to the 3Rs than reading, writing and arithmetic. The message of reduce, reuse and recycle is now taught in schools with as much vigour as the other basics. Along with this focus on the environment comes increased scrutiny of the schools' own environmental practices. One result is that a number of schools are starting to compost right where compostable waste is produced — on the school grounds.

Alcott Elementary School in Concord, Massachusetts, for example, was one of the first schools in the United States to start a food waste composting program. During the 1990 school year, over 3,000 pounds of food, paper napkins and lunch bags were composted.

Not only does this reduce the amount of garbage being thrown away, but more important it gets students directly involved in environmental solutions. At school composting projects, students are often the people assigned to look after the compost pile and in the process they learn about the science of soil and the recycling of nutrients.

Some schools are taking it even further — producing finished compost to be used on the school garden. A non-profit group called City Farmer, based in Vancouver, British Columbia, promotes the idea of city food gardening, and in 1986 they helped create a children's food garden at Lord Roberts Elementary School. Such projects also exist throughout the United States, and educators have found that school gardens are an excellent tool for teaching environmental studies and the life sciences.

Vermicomposting at School

Worm bins in the classroom are an excellent way to teach kids about composting, and the idea of hundreds of wigglers inside the school is particularly appealing to kids. (And, of course, teachers could also have worm bins in the teachers' lounge.) Activities for the students could include constructing their own worm bin, weighing the amount of food waste put into the bin, counting the number of worms in the bin after a month to see how the numbers have grown, monitoring which food wastes break down fastest in the worm bin, researching about worms and their ecology, comparing the health of potted plants that have been enriched with worm castings as opposed to potted plants in regular soil (or even comparing a worm-casting-enriched corner of the schoolyard with a regular patch of grass in the schoolyard).

A COMPOST RIDDLE FOR KIDS
What's three feet by three feet by three feet, sits in your backyard and acts like a low maintenance pet?
    What sits on your balcony and eats about thirty percent of your garbage?
    What looks like an out-of-the-way storage box but turns your organic garbage into garden gold?
    Yes, you guessed it — a compost container!

TEACHING COMPOST BASICS

Once kids are interested in composting, you can teach them the basic rules for producing good compost: adequate air in the pile, enough moisture, and a good mix of materials. A useful experiment is to make a few mini-piles, some the wrong way and some the right way, and to compare the results.

For example, you could set up four composting buckets and keep them outside:

- One without enough nitrogen: Use only dried brown leaves in this pile. Moisten but do not soak the leaves. Turn over every few days.
- One without enough moisture: Use dried leaves, vegetable and fruit waste. Do not moisten. Turn over every few days.
- One without enough air circulation: Use dried leaves, vegetable and fruit waste. Moisten but do not turn the materials.
- One with an ideal balance of materials, air and water: Use dried leaves, vegetable and fruit waste. Moisten. Turn over every few days.

After about three weeks, compare the results in the different buckets. Did one bucket produce darker, crumblier compost that looks more like soil than the others? Did any of the buckets start to smell? Can you recognize any of the original materials that went into any of the buckets?

At the end of this experiment, kids will know what makes a healthy heap and what doesn't work.

AFTERWORD

Dirty Hands, Clean Conscience

"Political composting" suggests a convenient way to dispose of (indeed, to break down) politicians' rhetoric. But that's not quite what we're referring to. Instead, we're talking about the political future and possibilities of composting throughout North America. What type of future does composting have as a waste reduction tool? What kind of composting opportunities are there beyond the backyard?

If you've followed the suggestions contained in this book, you're probably composting happily in your backyard, balcony or basement, and you've probably been inspired, motivated and encouraged by the dramatic reduction in your garbage output. You've made a fine and laudable contribution to solving the garbage crisis. And if you're interested in doing even more good work, there are plenty of opportunities to promote composting in your community, plenty of opportunities to get involved.

Although many cities and towns have been enlightened about the benefits of composting as a waste reduction tool, there are still other communities that have not yet taken even the first small steps. For example, is your local government promoting composting by making compost bins available to residents at a reduced price or for free? Do your community politicians have a *vision* of a bin in every backyard? If not, you can get involved by phoning city hall, the public works department, your local representatives, the mayor, or by writing to local newspapers and radio stations. Armed with the information that subsidized or free compost bins have been proven to *save* cities money (by diverting garbage from rapidly overflowing landfill sites, reducing garbage volume and therefore garbage collection costs, reducing the volume of wastes that cities have to pay to put in landfill), you can spread the composting word convincingly.

In addition to home composting, how about exploring the possibilities of centralized composting (that is, a large composting facility run by the city) as a way of dealing with dead leaves from parks, food waste from government buildings and local businesses, etc. The finished compost produced by the facility could be made available to residents for beautifying yards and gardens. Many communities are already doing this.

Does your local government promote composting by providing educational materials to the public? Do your schools educate children about composting by having a bin right on school property? Does your daycare facility compost? Does your office have a worm bin in the lunchroom or cafeteria? There are many ways to get people involved in and enthused about composting. How about getting a local official or celebrity with a high public profile interested in composting and organize a media event around the christening of her or his bin? Do the U.S. president, the Canadian prime minister, the provincial premiers, the state governors all have compost bins? Let's start asking. Spread the word. Make change happen.

Glossary

Acidic: The opposite of alkaline; having a pH reading of below 7.
Aeration: Getting oxygen into the compost pile.
Aerobic Bacteria: Bacteria that require oxygen.
African Night Crawler: A variety of worm suitable for vermicomposting.
Alkaline: The opposite of acidic; having a pH reading of above 7.
Anaerobic Bacteria: Bacteria that work only in the absence of oxygen.

Bedding Material: Material used as the organic medium for composting with worms.
Biodegradable Materials: Materials that will break down and decompose.
Browns: Compost materials that are high in carbon.

Carbon:Nitrogen Ratio: The ratio of carbon to nitrogen in an organic substance.
Compost: The end result of composting — a dark, rich conditioner that looks like soil.
Compost Activators: High-nitrogen materials that get your compost pile working quickly.
Compost Heap: An unenclosed compost pile (not held in with any structure).
Compost Starters: High-nitrogen materials that get your compost pile working quickly.
Compost Tea: Water in which compost has been mixed.

Compostable Materials: Organic materials that will decompose in a compost pile.

Composting: The breaking down or decomposition of organic matter by a community of micro-organisms, known as decomposer organisms, into a nutrient-rich soil conditioner. In a backyard or balcony, composting is the speeding up of a natural decomposition process under the semi-controlled conditions of a heap, pile or bin.

Cover Crops: Plants such as clover and rye that are grown specifically to be ploughed under, before maturity, to enrich the soil.

Decomposer Organism: An organism that breaks down matter into simpler substances.

Decomposition: The process of breaking down organic materials into their component parts or basic elements.

Dew Worm: A worm variety, commonly found in gardens and harvested from golf courses, that is *not* appropriate for vermicomposting.

Fertilizer: A substance (natural or synthetic) used to enrich the soil.

Green Manure: Fresh, green plant material dug into the soil. Green plant material is high in nitrogen, which is released by the soil bacteria that decompose the green material.

Greens: Compost materials that are high in nitrogen.

Humus: The end product of composting; the organic matter that results from the decomposition of plant and animal matter. Humus holds and slowly releases nutrients and trace elements to plants as they need them for growth.

Inoculants: Specially prepared mixtures of bacterial cultures to add to your pile.

Leaf Mould: Decomposed or partly decomposed leaves.

Manure Worm: A worm variety suitable for vermicomposting.

Maturation Stage: The final stage in a compost pile.

Mesophilic Bacteria: Bacteria that work at medium to high temperatures.

Micro-organism: An organism that is not visible to the human eye.

Mulch: A layer of (usually undecomposed organic) material put on top of the soil.

Non-biodegradable Materials: Materials that will not break down and decompose.

Organic Matter: Anything that is, or once was, living.

Pathogens: Disease-causing organisms.

Pest-proofing: Making it impossible for animals to invade your compost bin or pile.

pH: A measure of a substance's alkalinity or acidity.

Plant Nutrients: The chemicals that plants require in order to grow. The major plant nutrients are nitrogen, phosphorus and potassium.

Psychrophilic Bacteria: Bacteria that work at low temperatures.

Redworm: A variety of worm suitable for vermicomposting.

Sidedressing: Digging compost or fertilizer into the soil around a plant.

Soil Conditioner: Something that improves the physical condition of soil and increases its organic content.

Soil Incorporation: Burying material in soil, where it decomposes.

Synthetic Chemicals: Chemicals that are manufactured by humans.

Thermophilic Bacteria: Bacteria that work at high temperatures.
Trace Elements: Chemicals that plants need in small quantities in order to grow.

Ventilation: Getting oxygen into the compost pile.
Ventilation Stack: Any kind of tubing (usually perforated) put in a compost pile to ensure adequate air supply.
Vermicompost: The end result of composting with worms, vermicompost contains worm castings as well as decomposed organic matter.
Vermicomposter: Bin designed specifically for composting with worms.
Vermicomposting: Composting with worms.
Volatilization: Rapid evaporation.

Worm Castings: Worm manure, materials that have passed through the worm's digestive tract and mixed with mucus.

Sources

BOOKS
On Composting:
Composting: A Study of the Process and its Principles by Clarence G. Golueke, Rodale Press, Emmaus, Pennsylvania, 1972.
Ecology of Compost by Daniel L. Dindal, State University of New York, Syracuse, New York, 1976.
Let It Rot! The Home Gardener's Guide to Composting by Stu Campbell, Garden Way Publishing, Pownal, Vermont, 1975.
Rodale Book of Composting: Easy Methods for Every Gardener edited by Grace Gershuny and Deborah L. Martin, Rodale Press, Emmaus, Pennsylvania, 1992.

On Vermicomposting:
The Earthworm Book by Jerry Minnich, Rodale Press, Emmaus, Pennsylvania, 1977.
Worms Eat My Garbage by Mary Appelhof, Flower Press, 10332 Shaver Road, Kalamazoo, Michigan 49002, 1982.

On Mulching:
How to Have a Green Thumb Without an Aching Back by Ruth Stout, Simon and Schuster, New York, New York, 1987.
The Mulch Book by Stu Campbell, Garden Way Publishing, Pownal, Vermont, 1991.

On Building Your Own Bin:
Homemade: 101 Easy-to-Make Things for Your Garden,

Home, or Farm by Ken Braren and Roger Griffith, Garden Way Publishing, Pownal, Vermont, 1977.

The Smart Kitchen: How to Design a Comfortable, Safe, Energy-Efficient, and Environmentally-Friendly Workspace by David Goldbeck, Ceres Press, Woodstock, New York, 1989.

On Garbage:

The Recycler's Handbook by Earthworks Group, Earthworks Press, Berkeley, California, 1990.

Rush to Burn: Solving America's Garbage Crisis? Newsday Staff, Island Press, Washington, D.C., 1989.

War on Waste: Can America Win Its Battle With Garbage? by Louis Blumberg and Robert Gottlieb, Island Press, Washington, D.C., 1989.

On Soil:

An Agricultural Testament by Sir A. Howard, Oxford University Press, Oxford, England, 1940.

Dirt by John Anthony Adams, Texas A & M Press, College Station, Texas, 1986.

Fundamentals of Soil Science by Henry D. Foth, John Wiley & Sons, New York, New York, 1978.

The Microbiology of Terrestrial Ecosystems by B.N. Richards, John Wiley & Sons, New York, New York, 1987.

Out of the Earth: Civilization and the Life of the Soil by Daniel J. Hillel, Macmillan, New York, New York, 1990.

Soil Biology Guide edited by Daniel L. Dindal, John Wiley & Sons, New York, New York, 1990.

The Soul of Soil: A Guide to Ecological Soil Management by Grace Gershuny and Joseph Smillie, Gaia Services, Erie, Quebec, 1986.

On Gardening Without Chemicals:

The Basic Book of Organic Gardening edited by Robert Rodale, Ballantine, New York, 1987.

Building Healthy Gardens by Catherine Osgood Foster, Garden Way, Charlotte, Vermont, 1989.

Building a Healthy Lawn by Stuart Franklin, Garden Way, Charlotte, Vermont, 1988.

The Chemical-Free Lawn by Warren Schultz, Rodale Press, Emmaus, Pennsylvania, 1989.

Ecological Gardening: Your Path to a Healthy Garden by Marjorie Harris, Random House, Toronto, Ontario, 1991.

Fertile Soil, agAccess, 603 Fourth Street, Davis, California 95616; (916) 756-7177.

A Greener Thumb by Mark Cullen, Penguin, Markham, Ontario, 1990.

The Harrowsmith Northern Gardener by Jennifer Bennett, Camden House, Camden East, Ontario, 1982.

For Kids:

Canadian Garbage Collectors by Paulette Bourgeois, Kids Can Press, Toronto, Ontario, 1991.

Earth Book for Kids by Linda Schwartz, The Learning Works Inc., Santa Barbara, California, 1990.

Earthcycles and Ecosystems by Beth Savan, Kids Can Press, Toronto, Ontario, 1991.

Make a Difference: Student Activities for a Better Environment by T. Ellis and T. Scanlan, Is Five Press, Toronto, Ontario, 1989.

Pee Wee and the Magical Compost Heap by Larraine Roulston, Recycling Resource Service, 527 Broadgreen Street, Pickering, Ontario L1W E38; (416) 420-5625.

Trash Attack! by Candace Savage, Douglas & McIntyre, Vancouver, British Columbia, 1990.

Worms Eat Our Garbage: Classroom Activities for a Better Environment by Mary Appelhof, Mary Frances Fenton, and Barbara Loss Harris, Flower Press, 10332 Shaver Road, Kalamazoo, Michigan 49002; (616) 327-0108.

Zebo and the Dirty Planet by Kim Fernandes, Annick Press, Toronto, Ontario, 1991.

MAGAZINES

On Composting and Garbage:

BioCycle: Journal of Composting and Recycling, JG Press, Box 351, 419 State Avenue, Emmaus, Pennsylvania 18049.

The Composters' Journal, Recycling Council of Ontario, 489 College Street, Suite 504, Toronto, Ontario M6G 1A5.

Municipal Solid Waste News, The Solid Waste Association of North America, Box 7219, Silver Spring, Maryland 20910.

Recycling Today, 4012 Bridge Avenue, Cleveland, Ohio 44113.

Reusable News, U.S. Environmental Protection Agency, 401 M Street S.W., Washington, D.C. 20460.

Waste Age, National Solid Wastes Management Association, Suite 1000, 1730 Rhode Island Avenue N.W., Washington, D.C. 20036.

Waste Matters, Solid Waste Management Division, Metropolitan Toronto Works Department, 439 University Avenue, 20th Floor, Toronto, Ontario M5G 1Y8.

Waste Not: The Weekly Reporter for Rational Resource Management, Work on Waste, 82 Judson, Canton, New York 13617.

Wastelines, Environmental Action Foundation, 6930 Carroll Avenue, Suite 600, Takoma Park, Maryland 20912.

On Vermicomposting:

The Wormletter (a quarterly newsletter on vermicomposting), #202—20 Cosburn Avenue, Toronto, Ontario M4K 2E7; (416) 423-4971.

For Educators:

Green Teacher, 95 Robert Street, Toronto, Ontario M5S 2K5.

On Municipal Composting:

BioCycle: Journal of Composting and Recycling, Box 351, 419 State Avenue, Emmaus, Pennsylvania 18049.

Waste Age, Suite 1000, 1730 Rhode Island Avenue N.W., Washington, D.C. 20036.

On Gardening:
COGnition, Canadian Organic Growers, Box 6408, Station J, Ottawa, Ontario K2A 3Y6.
Flower and Garden, 4251 Pennsylvania, Kansas City, Missouri 64111-9990.
Organic Gardening, Rodale Press, 33 East Minor Street, Emmaus, Pennsylvania 18098.

GROUPS FOR INFORMATION ON COMPOSTING
American Horticultural Society, 7931 East Boulevard Drive, Alexandria, Virginia 22308-1300; (703) 768-5700.

Canadian Organic Growers, Box 6408, Station J, Ottawa, Ontario K2A 3Y6.

City Farmer, #801 – 318 Homer Street, Vancouver, British Columbia V6B 2V3; (604) 685-5832.

Ecological Agriculture Projects, Box 191, Macdonald College, Ste. Anne de Bellevue, Quebec H9X 1C0; (514) 398-7771.

Ecology Action Centre, 3115 Veith Street, Halifax, Nova Scotia B3K 3G9; (902) 454-7828.

Ecology Center, 2350 San Pablo Avenue, Berkeley, California 94702; (415) 548-2220.

Environmental Action Foundation, 6930 Carrol Avenue, Suite 600, Takoma Park, Maryland 20912; (301) 891-1100.

Environmental Defense Fund, 257 Park Avenue South, New York, New York 10010; (212) 505-2100.

Fonds québécois de recupération, 407, boulevard St. Laurent, Suite 500, Montreal, Quebec H2Y 2V5; (514) 874-3701.

The Fort Whyte Centre for Environmental Education, 1961 McCreary Road, Winnipeg, Manitoba R3Y 1G5; (204) 895-7001.

Institute for Local Self-Reliance, 2425 – 18th Street N.W., Washington, D.C. 20009; (202) 232-4108.

It's Not Garbage Coalition, 401 Richmond Street West, Suite 104, Toronto, Ontario M5V 3A8; (416) 348-9696.

Recycling Council of Alberta, 3415 Ogden Road S.E., Calgary, Alberta T2G 4N4; (403) 262-4542.

Recycling Council of British Columbia, 2150 Maple Street, Vancouver, British Columbia V6J 3T3; (604) 731-7222.

Recycling Council of Manitoba, 412 McDermott Avenue, Winnipeg, Manitoba R3A 0A5; (204) 942-7781.

Recycling Council of Ontario, 489 College Street, Suite 504, Toronto, Ontario M6G 1A5; (416) 960-1025.

Rodale Institute, 222 Main Street, Emmaus, Pennsylvania 18098; (215) 967-5171.

Saskatchewan Environmental Society, 103-219 – 22nd Street East, Saskatoon, Saskatchewan S7K 3N9; (306) 665-1915.

Seattle Tilth Association, 4649 Sunnyside Avenue North, Seattle, Washington 98103; (206) 633-0451.

GROUPS FOR INFORMATION ON MUNICIPAL COMPOSTING
The Composting Council, 114 South Pitt Street, Alexandria, Virginia 22314; (703) 739-2401.

The Composting Council of Canada, 200 MacLaren Street, Ottawa, Ontario K2P 0L9; (613) 238-4014.

Cornell University, Resource Center-GP, 7 Business and Technology Park, Ithaca, New York 14850.

COMPUTER SOURCES
SWICH: The Solid Waste Information Clearing House (SWICH) library is available on electronic bulletin board; listing of 6,000 journals, reports, studies, etc.; created by the Governmental Refuse Collection and Disposal Association; call 1-800-67-SWICH.

VIDEO SOURCES
The Magic of Composting: available from the Recycling Council of Ontario, 489 College Street, Suite 504, Toronto, Ontario M6G 1A5; (416) 960-1025.
Recycling Within Reach: Wastewise; and *Yard Waste Composting for Municipalities:* available from Cornell University, Distribution Center, 7-8 Cornell Business and Technology Park, Ithaca, New York 14850; (607) 255-2091.

COMPOSTING AND EDUCATION (INFORMATION FOR SCHOOLS)
Cornell University, Resource Center-GP, 7 Business and Technology Park, Ithaca, New York 14850.

City Farmer, #801 – 318 Homer Street, Vancouver, British Columbia V6B 2V3; (604) 685-5832.

Educational Materials:
Composting: Wastes to Resources, Cornell Cooperative Extension, Distribution Centre-GP, 7 Business and Technology Park, Cornell University, Ithaca, New York 14850.

The Decomposer Food Web, by Daniel L. Dindal, Biocycle, Box 351, Emmaus, Pennsylvania 18049.

Earth Day Every Day: Waste Management: A Teacher's Resource, by Evannah Sakamoto and Janice Gershman, McGraw-Hill Ryerson, Toronto, Ontario, 1991.

Here Today Here Tomorrow, New Jersey Department of Environmental Protection, Trenton, New Jersey, 1989.

Here's the Dirt (video for libraries and schools), 4330 Kingsway, Burnaby, British Columbia V5H 4G8.

Recycle Saurous (recycling educational and promotional products), catalogue available from Creative Printing and Publishing, 757 N. Hwy. 17-92, Suite 104, Longwood, Florida 32750.

The Rotten Truth (video for kids and families), 50 Leyland Drive, Leonia, New Jersey 07605.

School Cafeteria Waste Composting: Suggested System Design, Recycling Section, Division of Solid Waste Management, 103 S. Main Street, Waterbury, Vermont 05676.

School Garden Guidelines, City Farmer, #801 — 318 Homer Street, Vancouver, British Columbia V6B 2V3.

Solid Waste Management Education Kit, Metropolitan Toronto Works Department, Toronto, Ontario, 1989.

Teaching Green: A Parent's Guide to Education for Life on Earth, by Damian Randle, Green Print, London, England, 1990.

HOME COMPOSTING BIN MANUFACTURERS AND DISTRIBUTORS (a partial list)

AL-KO Kober Corporation, 25784 Borg Road, Elkhart, Indiana 46514; (219) 264-0631.

American Horticultural Society, Composting Supplies, 7931 East Boulevard Drive, Alexandria, Virginia 22308-1300; (703) 768-5700; (800) 777-7931.

Barclay Recycling Inc., 75 Ingram Drive, Toronto, Ontario M6M 2M2; (416) 240-8227.

Bio Industries, Inc., 450 S. Lombard Road, Addison, Illinois 60101; (708) 953-8999.

CanDo Composter, 5990 Old Stilesboro Road, Acworth, Georgia 30101; (404) 974-0046.

Century Plastics, Ltd., 12291 Horseshoe Way, Richmond, British Columbia V7A 4V5; (604) 271-1324.

Composting Systems, Box 1507, Belleville, Ontario K8N 5J2; (613) 966-3727.

Crary Co., Box 849, West Fargo, North Dakota 58078; 1-800-247-7335.

Dalen Products, 11110 Gilbert Drive, Knoxville, Tennessee 37932; (615) 966-3256.

Eco Atlantic, Inc., 2200-C Broening Hwy., Baltimore, Maryland 21224; (401) 633-7500.

Environ-Mate Inc., Box 55521, 629 Markham Road, Scarborough, Ontario M1H 2A0; (416) 438-2548.

Environmental Applied Products, 2029 N. 23rd Street, Boise, Idaho 83702; (208) 368-7900.

Gardener's Supply Company, 128 Intervale Road, Burlington, Vermont 05401; (802) 863-1700; 1-800-876-5520.

Iron & Oak, 119 E. Front Street, Annawan, Illinois 61234; (309) 935-6353.

Kemp Company, 160 Koser Road, Lititz, Pennsylvania 17543; (717) 627-7979.

Kinsman Company, Inc., River Road, Point Pleasant, Pennsylvania 18950; (215) 297-5613.

Natursoil Company, 1930 9th Avenue SE, St. Cloud, Minnesota 56301; (612) 252-6255.

Obex Inc., Box 1253, Stamford, Connecticut 06901; (203) 975-9094.

Ringer Corporation, 9959 Valley View Road, Eden Prairie, Minnesota 55344; (612) 941-4180; 1-800-654-1047.

Smith & Hawken, 25 Corte Madera, Mill Valley, California 94941; (415) 381-1800.

Solar Cone, P.O. Box 67, Seward, Illinois 61077-0067; (815) 247-8454.

Troy-Bilt Manufacturing Company, 102nd Street and 9th Avenue, Troy, New York 12180; (518) 235-6010; 1-800-833-6990.

Vision Recycling, 7005 Taschereau Boulevard, Brossard, Quebec J4Z 1A7; (514) 926-4120.

HEAT FROM COMPOST
Nature's Way Inc., "Compost Plus," 3833 S. 24th Street, Omaha, Nebraska 68107; (402) 734-2465.

COMPOST SIEVE:
Gardener's Supply, 128 Intervale Road, Burlington, Vermont 05401; (802) 863-1700.

KITCHEN COLLECTORS:
Gardener's Eden, Box 7307, San Francisco, California 94120-7307; (800) 822-9600.

COMPOST TEA MAKER:
Plow & Hearth, Box 830, 301 Madison Avenue, Orange, Virginia 22960; (703) 672-1712; 1-800-627-1712.

WORM SOURCES
Bait farms are listed in the Yellow Pages. Look under "Bait," "Fishing Supplies" and "Worms." As well, many stores that specialize in environmental products sell worms for vermicomposting. If you're having trouble finding an eco-source, call a local environmental group or recycling organization.

B & P, Box 398, Olathe, Colorado 81425; (303) 323-6550.

The Canadian Original Vermicomposter Ltd., 507 King Street East, Unit #18, Toronto, Ontario M5A 1M3; (416) 366-8674.

Cape Cod Worm Farm, 30 Center Avenue, Buzzards Bay, Massachusetts 02532; (508) 759-5664.

Dirt Cheap Organics, 5645 Paradise Drive, Corte Madera, California 94925; (415) 924-0369.

Early Bird Ecology and Bait Farms, RR#1, Smithville, Ontario L0R 2A0; (416) 643-4251.

Flowerfield Enterprises, 10332 Shaver Road, Kalamazoo, Michigan 49002; (616) 327-0108.

Gardener's Supply Company, 128 Intervale Road, Burlington, Vermont 05401; (802) 863-1700; (800) 876-5520.

Good Earth Organics, 570 Brevard Road, Asheville, North Carolina 28806; (704) 252-4414.

Seattle Tilth Association, 4649 Sunnyside Avenue North, Seattle, Washington 98103; (206) 633-0451.

VERMICOMPOSTER SOURCES

The Canadian Original Vermicomposter Ltd., 507 King Street East, Unit #18, Toronto, Ontario M5A 1M3; (416) 366-8674.

Flowerfield Enterprises, 10332 Shaver Road, Kalamazoo, Michigan 49002; (616) 327-0108.

Gardener's Supply Company, 128 Intervale Road, Burlington, Vermont 05401; (802) 863-1700; (800) 876-5520.

Smith & Hawken, 25 Corte Madera, Mill Valley, California 94941; (415) 381-1800.

We Recycle Corporation, Box 447, 342 Bronte Street South, Milton, Ontario L9T 5B7; (416) 875-2588.

MUNICIPAL COMPOSTING
Books and Reports:

Beyond 40 Percent, Institute for Local Self Reliance, 2425 18th Street N.W., Washington, D.C. 20009; 1990.

The BioCycle Guide to the Art & Science of Composting, edited by the staff of *BioCycle Journal of Waste Recycling*, BioCycle, Emmaus, Pennsylvania, 1991.

Seattle Tilth Association, 4649 Sunnyside Avenue North, Seattle, Washington 98103; (206) 633-0451.

The Worm Factory, 129 Sherbrooke Street East, Perth, Ontario K7H 3B1; (613) 267-5540.

The Worm Farm, 31 Herman Avenue, Toronto, Ontario M6R 1Y1; (416) 588-5280.

VERMICOMPOSTER SOURCES

The Canadian Original Vermicomposter Ltd., 507 King Street East, Unit #18, Toronto, Ontario M5A 1M3; (416) 366-8674.

Earthworm Environmental Services, 1284 Humberside Drive, Kingston, Ontario K7P 2N1; (613) 634-0315.

Simply Better Environmental Products, 3 Strathcona Avenue, Toronto, Ontario M4K 1K6; (416) 462-9599.

We Recycle Corporation, Box 447, 342 Bronte Street South, Milton, Ontario L9T 5B7; (416) 875-2588.

The Worm Factory, 129 Sherbrooke Street East, Perth, Ontario K7H 3B1; (613) 267-5540.

MUNICIPAL COMPOSTING
Books and Reports:

Beyond 40 Percent, Institute for Local Self Reliance, 2425 18th Street N.W., Washington, D.C. 20009; 1990.

The BioCycle Guide to the Art & Science of Composting, edited by the staff of *BioCycle Journal of Waste Recycling*, BioCycle, Emmaus, Pennsylvania, 1991.

The BioCycle Guide to Composting Municipal Wastes, edited by the staff of *BioCycle Journal of Waste Recycling*, BioCycle, Emmaus, Pennsylvania, 1989.

The BioCycle Guide to Yard Waste Composting, edited by the staff of *BioCycle Journal of Waste Recycling*, BioCycle, Emmaus, Pennsylvania, 1990.

Municipal Composting: Resources for Local Officials and Community Organizations, Institute for Local Self Reliance, 2425 18th Street N.W., Washington, D.C. 20009; 1980.

Sensible Sludge: A New Look at a Wasted Natural Resource, by Jerome Goldstein, Rodale Press, Emmaus, Pennsylvania, 1977.

Index